BY PHILIP GUEDALLA

———

JUVENILIA
    IGNES FATUI: a Book of Parodies.
    METRI GRATIA: Verse and Prose

ESSAYS
    MASTERS AND MEN.
    A GALLERY.
    SUPERS AND SUPERMEN.

HISTORY
    THE PARTITION OF EUROPE: a Text-Book of European History, 1715-
        1815.
    THE SECOND EMPIRE.

POLITICS
    THE INDUSTRIAL FUTURE: a Liberal Policy.

SUPERS AND SUPERMEN

SUPERS & SUPERMEN

BY

PHILIP GUEDALLA

❧

G.P. Putnam's Sons
New York & London
The Knickerbocker Press
1924

The
Knickerbocker
Press
New York

Made in the United States of America

To

N. OR M.

BUT

IN EITHER CASE

TO

MY WIFE

NOTE

To me this little book is all that the Santa Maria *was to Columbus. For in it I discovered America. The opportunity of a new edition permits me to acknowledge the increasing interest of that discovery; to make a complete revision of the text; and to include four papers—those on* Some Ambassadors, Some Rich Men, P. T. Barnum, *and* The Irish Guards—*which have not yet appeared in any volume.*

P. G.

CONTENTS

SUPERS

SUPERMEN

I. GENTLEMEN ADVENTURERS

CONTENTS

II. PRIMITIVES

IN MEMORIAM

SUPERS AND SUPERMEN

SUPERS

Some Foreign Secretaries
Some Historians
Some Strategists
Some Critics
Some Ambassadors
Some Frenchmen
Some More Frenchmen
Some Zionists
Some Germans
Some Romans
Some Literary Men
Some Turks
Some Serbs
Some Peers—
    I. Lord Russell
    II. Lord Wellesley
    III. Lord North
    IV. Lords Lyons and Clarendon
Some Lawyers
Some Rich Men
Some Revolutionaries
An American

SOME FOREIGN SECRETARIES

WHISPERING from its towers the last enchantment
of the middle-class, the Foreign Office occupies an
eligible central situation between Whitehall and St.
James's Park. The grateful taxpayer provides it
with an abundance of admirable stationery, and it is
perhaps the last place in London where everybody
is a gentleman. Possibly that is why it is deficient
in repartee and finds its strength, like the well-bred
heroes of Mr. Seton Merriman, in silence. It is, like
that other cause of revolutions, the States-General of
1789, an interesting but neglected antiquity, hovering
uncertainly between an uncomfortable club for
elderly bachelors and an academy for the sons of
gentlemen (for at least one grandfather is the legal
minimum). Behind the solid joinery of its doors,
and above the royal ciphers upon its hearth-rugs, the
public acts of the United Kingdom lie in the hands
of fifty persons and at the mercy of about five.

The Foreign Office, as Lord Avebury must have
said of Stonehenge, is a remarkable place. For the

3

average Englishman it occupies a position a little
higher than the Post Office, a little lower than the
Bank. But among all the public institutions of Great
Britain it has impressed the Continent. It has impressed it almost as profoundly as the Lord-
Mayoralty and the sale of wives at Smithfield. An
historian of the Second Empire, whose election to the
French Academy did not depend solely upon his
philology, has referred with reverence to the subtlety
of the *Forig Office de Londres,* and his respect is
typical of its European reputation. The causes of
this sentiment are among the most mysterious things
in Europe. It may be the quality of its notepaper
(which is excellent), since it can hardly be the continuity of its policy, which is not continuous.

Through the whole course of history Great Britain
has consistently confounded her enemies by the inconsistency of her acts. Latin logic and Teutonic deduction have exhausted the exactitude of all the
systems in the effort to forecast the proceedings of
British statesmen. But there is no calculation known
to man that can discover the next move of England,
since it is never known to England itself. To this is
due the Puck-like quality of His Majesty's Principal
Secretaries of State. That is the essence of British
policy; it has no golden rule except that it has no
golden rule. It proceeds in no single ascertained

4

direction for ten years at a time; that is where it gets the better of Russian policy, which laboriously executed through the Nineteenth Century the codicils of the will of Peter the Great. It seeks no natural frontiers, because geography is not taught in the Public Schools; that is where it has the advantage over France, which is perpetually returning, as any schoolboy can see, to the line of the Rhine. It has no natural enmities comparable to the rivalry of Slav and Teuton, because the European Powers have been indifferently its allies and its adversaries. In the result British policy has remained the incalculable factor which does the sum, whilst the movement of Russia towards the Dardanelles, of France towards the Rhine, or of Germany towards the lower Scheldt was patent to anyone who could read a line of history or a square inch of a map. It is a great inheritance. For three centuries Great Britain has maintained the stupendous opportunism of the Balance of Power, facing the European storm with a variation of direction and an accuracy of judgment which were both borrowed from the weather-cock. As a national symbol that prescient and revolving fowl may lack inspiration, but it represents fairly enough the starry ideal to which British statesmanship has hitched the waggon of British policy. "It is a narrow policy to suppose that this country or that is to be marked out as the eternal ally or the perpetual enemy of England. We have no eternal allies, and we have no perpetual enemies. Our interests are eternal and perpetual, and those interests it is our duty to follow." The statement is no less reliable because it was made by Lord Palmerston following a considered judgment of Mr. Canning. If he had known French (an accomplishment normally confined to permanent officials) the noble lord might have said of his country's policy: *Plus ça change, plus c'est la même chose.*

One fascinating result of this constant variation of direction is a delightful inconsistency between its various exponents. Right honourable gentlemen stretch quivering forefingers across the despatch box towards the wrath to come, and locate it alternately in North and South and East. Spain, Holland, France, Russia and Germany have successively troubled the sleep of British Ministers, and it is remarkable that Austria is the one country in Europe that has never provided England with a menace. In these circumstances, it was delightfully malicious of a friend of Mr. Lloyd George to compile an anthology of speeches on British policy. These Little Flowers of the Foreign Office are so engagingly divergent; it is a garden which grows, after a celebrated model, quite contrary. Any collection of speeches which is largely Parliamentary is consequently disfigured with the wealth of unnecessary parenthesis which forms the House of Commons manner. One can never forget that Robinson in his embarrassed transit through English politics embellished one Budget speech with a series of six visions and a quotation from Shakespeare and ended another with a sentence standing twenty-seven lines long in Hansard. Even Foreign Secretaries are more reasonable when they get to the country, and the finest speeches in the collection are those delivered to popular audiences. It is a most useful and instructive garner; it might perhaps be called the Brazen Treasury.

It is hardly kind to the memory of Chatham to include a speech on the Spanish question delivered in Opposition; any man was justified in talking nonsense to get Walpole out of office. But his second speech, which derives a false appearance of relevance from its title, "The Defence of Weaker States," contains an interesting, if unconscious, prophecy:

With respect to Corsica I shall only say that France has obtained a more useful and important acquisition in one pacific campaign than in any of her belligerent campaigns.

The noble Earl was speaking in the year 1770. Six months earlier by the act of policy to which he referred a child of uncertain temper called Napoleon came into the world as a French subject: it was a French acquisition of which the precise extent was to be fully appreciated by Chatham's son. The wise compiler would include comparatively few of the innumerable speeches inspired by the really Great War; there should be the admirable onslaughts of Sheridan upon the traditional system of fighting British battles with the hire-purchase armies of Hesse-Cassel, "the *posse comitatus,* the rabble of Germany"; and there will no doubt come an interminable speech by William Pitt on the unreliable diplomacy of the Consulate, closing with the celebrated *"Cur igitur pacem nolo? Quia infida est, quia periculosa, quia esse non potest,"* an apostrophe which would leave the present House of Commons under the impression that peace had been concluded upon terms which it was inadvisable at the present moment to divulge.

There is no clearer statement of England's claim to act as the Special Constable of Europe than Palmerston's Polish speech of 1848:

I hold that the real policy of England—apart from questions which involve her own particular interests, political or commercial—is to be the champion of justice and right; pursuing that course with moderation and prudence, not becoming the Quixote of the world, but giving the weight of

her moral sanction and support wherever she thinks that
justice is, and wherever she thinks that wrong has been done.

It is surprising that no contemporary seems to
have noticed the quaint humour of this statement
of policy by a country without an army.

Perhaps the most instructive pieces in the collection are the speeches delivered by Earl Russell
and Mr. Disraeli in 1864 upon the Austro-Prussian
invasion of Denmark. The Treaty of London had
undoubtedly placed Great Britain under certain obli-
gations with regard to Danish integrity. The Prussians had occupied Schleswig-Holstein and driven
the Danes behind the lines of Düppel. But "my
Lords, our honour not being engaged, we have to
consider what we might be led to do for the interests
of other Powers, and for the sake of that balance of
power which in 1852 was declared by general consent to be connected with the integrity of Denmark.
. . . In the first place, is it the duty of this country—
if we are to undertake the preservation of the balance
of power in Europe as it was recognized in 1852—
is it a duty incumbent on us alone?" This argument
was supplemented a week later by Mr. Disraeli, when
he informed another place that "under that Treaty
England incurred no legal responsibility which was
not equally entered into by France and by Russia."

9

These speeches are a mine of unheroic but ingenious argument, with which Ministers of the Crown might have defended the non-intervention of England in the war for Belgium. They were explained two years later, when Lord Stanley expounded after Sadowa "the feeling that we ought not to be dragged into these Continental wars," and added that "if North Germany is to become a single Great Power, I do not see that any English interest is in the least degree affected"; it must be remembered that the noble Lord was at that date sleepless with the fear of French *chassepots* and the military efficiency of the Second Empire.

But the brightest jewel in the Downing Street coronal is the speech in which the Earl of Beaconsfield laid the Treaty of Berlin upon the table of the House of Lords. Disraeli at his worst was a political Perlmutter, and his ready-made formulæ never fitted his country worse. If his novels were always the novels of a politician, his politics were never more obviously the politics of a novelist. An accident of youth had taken the noble Earl upon a pleasure cruise in the Levant, and it resulted that forty years later his country was pledged to the sacred cause of Turkey. The Sikhs came to Malta, the Fleet went to Besika Bay, and Mr. Macdermott was understood to observe that the Russians should not have Constantinople. The Prime Minister agreed with him, and went to Berlin to say so: the result was that miracle of diplomatic ingenuity which Europe has been occupied in destroying for the last eight years.

My Lords, it has been said that no limit has been fixed to the occupation of Bosnia by Austria. Well, I think that was a very wise step.

There you have the elements of the annexation crisis of 1908 and the assassination of the Archduke Franz Ferdinand in 1914.

It is not the first time that Austria has occupied provinces at the request of Europe to ensure that order and tranquillity, which are European interests, might prevail in them. Not once, twice, or thrice has Austria undertaken such an office.

To the happy monuments of the Netherlands and North Italy Lord Beaconsfield gaily added Old Serbia: it is the problem before Europe to-day. With regard to Bulgaria he added with pride:

The new Principality, which was to exercise such an influence and produce a revolution in the disposition of the territory and policy of that part of the globe, is now merely a state in the Valley of the Danube, and both in its extent and population is reduced to one-third of what was contemplated by the Treaty of San Stefano.

That is the direct cause of the Balkan War, and when Turkey emerged shattered from that conflict

SUPERS AND SUPERMEN

Germany entered on the phase of disillusioned desperation which brought it to the mad-dog policy of the summer of 1914. It was a little bitter of the anthologist to reprint that speech in that year. Of the speeches provoked by the last war (or is it the last but one?) Mr. Asquith's, in addition to his successful negotiation of Mr. George Morrow's shibboleth "we are unsheathing our sword," were at once the shortest and the best. Viscount Grey was almost offensively simple: one cannot satisfactorily transpose all politics and half history into words of one syllable, and the dialect of Mrs. Markham is unsuited to the broad treatment of European problems. Mr. Lloyd George was more characteristic. The enemy were reviled as though they had been Unionists; and in the last round that ear, always so near to the ground, detected the coming boom in pugilism, and its master became the spokesman of Western Europe on the strength of a metaphor from the prize-ring.

It would be cruel to ask the editor of such a collection for an index, which must contain such entries as "Prussia, nobility of, p. 323; perfidy of, p. 537." Which is the best of the Balance of Power.

SOME HISTORIANS

It was Quintilian or Mr. Max Beerbohm who said, "History repeats itself: historians repeat each other." The saying is full of the mellow wisdom of either writer, and stamped with the peculiar veracity of the Silver Age of Roman or British epigram. One might have added, if the aphorist had stayed for an answer, that history is rather interesting when it repeats itself: historians are not. In France, which is an enlightened country enjoying the benefits of the Revolution and a public examination in rhetoric, historians are expected to write in a single and classical style of French. The result is sometimes a rather irritating uniformity; it is one long Taine that has no turning, and any quotation may be attributed with safety to Guizot, because *la nuit tous les chats sont gris.* But in England, which is a free country, the restrictions natural to ignorant (and immoral) foreigners are put off by the rough island race, and history is written in a dialect which is not curable by education, and cannot (it would seem) be prevented by injunction.

13

Historians' English is not a style; it is an industrial disease. The thing is probably scheduled in the Workmen's Compensation Act, and the publisher may be required upon notice of the attack to make a suitable payment to the writer's dependants. The workers in this dangerous trade are required to adopt (like Mahomet's coffin) a detached standpoint—that is, to write as if they took no interest in the subject. Since it is not considered good form for a graduate of less than sixty years' standing to write upon any period that is either familiar or interesting, this feeling is easily acquired, and the resulting narrations present the dreary impartiality of the Recording Angel without that completeness which is the sole attraction of his style. Wilde complained of Mr. Hall Caine that he wrote at the top of his voice; but a modern historian, when he is really detached, writes like someone talking in the next room, and few writers have equalled the chilly precision of Coxe's observation that the Turks "sawed the Archbishop and the Commandant in half, and committed other grave violations of international law."

Having purged his mind of all unsteadying interest in the subject, the young historian should adopt a moral code of more than Malthusian severity, which may be learned from any American writer of the last century upon the Renaissance or the decadence of

14

Spain. This manner, which is especially necessary in passages dealing with character, will lend to his work the grave dignity that is requisite for translation into Latin prose, that supreme test of an historian's style. It will be his misfortune to meet upon the byways of history the oddest and most abnormal persons, and he should keep by him (unless he wishes to forfeit his Fellowship) some convenient formula by which he may indicate at once the enormity of the subject and the disapproval of the writer. The writings of Lord Macaulay will furnish him at need with the necessary facility in lightning characterization. It was the practice of Cicero to label his contemporaries without distinction as "heavy men"; and the characters of history are easily divisible into "far-seeing statesmen" and "reckless libertines." It may be objected that although it is sufficient for the purposes of contemporary caricature to represent Mr. Gladstone as a collar or Mr. Chamberlain as an eye-glass, it is an inadequate record for posterity. But it is impossible for a busy man to write history without formulæ, and after all sheep are sheep and goats are goats. Lord Macaulay once wrote of someone, "In private life he was stern, morose, and inexorable": he was probably a Dutchman. It is a passage which has served as a lasting model for the historian's treatment of character. I had always imagined that

15

SUPERS AND SUPERMEN

Cliché was a suburb of Paris, until I discovered it to be a street in Oxford. Thus, if the working historian is faced with a period of "deplorable excesses," he handles it like a man, and writes always as if he was illustrated with steel engravings:

The imbecile king now ripened rapidly towards a crisis. Surrounded by a Court in which the inanity of the day was rivalled only by the debauchery of the night, he became incapable towards the year 1472 of distinguishing good from evil, a fact which contributed considerably to the effectiveness of his foreign policy, but was hardly calculated to conform with the monastic traditions of his House. Long nights of drink and dicing weakened a constitution that was already undermined, and the council-table, where once Campo Santo had presided, was disfigured with the despicable apparatus of Bagatelle. The burghers of the capital were horrified by the wild laughter of his madcap courtiers, and when it was reported in London that Ladislas had played at Halma, the Court of St. James's received his envoy in the deepest ceremonial mourning.

That is precisely how it is done. The passage exhibits the benign and contemporary influences of Lord Macaulay and Mr. Bowdler, and it contains all the necessary ingredients, except perhaps a "venal Chancellor" and a "greedy mistress." Vice is a subject of especial interest to historians, who are in most cases residents in small country towns; and there is unbounded truth in the rococo footnote of a writer on the Renaissance, who said *à propos* of a

Pope: "The disgusting details of his vices smack somewhat of the morbid historian's lamp." The note itself is a fine example of that concrete visualization of the subject which led Macaulay to observe that in consequence of Frederick's invasion of Silesia "black men fought on the coast of Coromandel and red men scalped each other by the Great Lakes of North America."

A less exciting branch of the historian's work is the reproduction of contemporary sayings and speeches. Thus, an obituary should always close on a note of regretful quotation:

He lived in affluence and died in great pain. "Thus," it was said by the most eloquent of his contemporaries, "thus terminated a career as varied as it was eventful, as strange as it was unique."

But for the longer efforts of sustained eloquence greater art is required. It is no longer usual, as in Thucydides' day, to compose completely new speeches, but it is permissible for the historian to heighten the colours and even to insert those rhetorical questions and complexes of personal pronouns which will render the translation of the passage into Latin prose a work of consuming interest and lasting profit:

The Duke assembled his companions for the forlorn hope, and addressed them briefly in *Oratio obliqua*. "His father," he said, "had always cherished in his heart the idea that he would one day return to his own people. Had he fallen in vain? Was it for nothing that they had dyed with their loyal blood the soil of a hundred battlefields? The past was dead, the future was yet to come. Let them remember that great sacrifices were necessary for the attainment of great ends, let them think of their homes and families, and if they had any pity for an exile, an outcast, and an orphan, let them die fighting."

That is the kind of passage that used to send the blood of Dr. Bradley coursing more quickly through his veins. The march of its eloquence, the solemnity of its sentiment, and the rich balance of its pronouns unite to make it a model for all historians: it can be adapted for any period.

It is hardly possible in a short study to include the special branches of the subject. Such are those efficient modern text-books, in which events are referred to either as "factors" (as if they were a sum) or as "phases" (as if they were the moon). There is also the solemn business of writing economic history, in which the historian may lapse at will into algebra, and anything not otherwise describable may be called "social tissue." A special subject is constituted by the early conquests of Southern and Central

America. In these there is a uniform opening for all passages which runs:

It was now the middle of October, and the season was drawing to an end. Soon the mountains would be whitened with the snows of winter and every rivulet swollen to a roaring torrent. Cortez, whose determination only increased with misfortune, decided to delay his march until the inclemency of the season abated. . . . It was now the middle of November, and the season was drawing to an end. . . .

There is, finally, the method of military history. This may be patriotic, technical, or in the manner prophetically indicated by Virgil as *Belloc, horrida Belloc*. The finest exponent of the patriotic style is undoubtedly the Rev. W. H. Fitchett, a distinguished colonial clergyman and historian of the Napoleonic wars. His night-attacks are more nocturnal, and his scaling parties are more heroically scaligerous than those of any other writer. His drummer-boys are the most moving in my limited circle of drummer-boys. One gathers that the Peninsular War abounded with pleasing incident of this type:

THE NIGHT ATTACK

It was midnight when Staff-Surgeon Pettigrew showed the flare from the summit of Sombrero. At once the whole plain was alive with the hum of the great assault. The four columns speedily got into position with flares and bugles at the head of each. One made straight for the Watergate, a second for the Bailey-guard, a third for the Porter-house, and the last (led by the saintly Smeathe) for the Tube station. Let us follow the second column on its secret mission through the night, lit by torches and cheered on by the huzzas of a thousand English throats. "—— the ——s," cried Cocker in a voice hoarse with patriotism; at that moment a red-hot shot hurtled over the plain and, ricocheting treacherously from the frozen river, dashed the heroic leader to the ground. Captain Boffskin, of the Buffs, leapt up with the dry coughing howl of the British infantryman. "—— them," he roared, "—— them to ——"; and for the last fifty yards it was neck and neck with the ladders. Our gallant drummer-boys laid to again, but suddenly a shot rang out from the silent ramparts. The 94th Léger were awake. *We were discovered!*

The war of 1870 required more special treatment. Its histories show no peculiar characteristic, but its appearances in fiction deserve special attention. There is a standard pattern:

How the Prussians came to Guitry-le-sec

It was a late afternoon in early September, or an early afternoon in late September—I forget these things—when I missed the boat express from Kerplouarnec to Pouzy-le-roi and was forced by the time-table to spend three hours at the forgotten hamlet of Guitry-le-sec, in the heart of Dauphiné. It contained besides a quantity of underfed poultry one white church, one white Mairie, and nine white houses. An old man with a white beard came towards me up the long white road. "It was on just such an afternoon as this forty years ago," he began, "that . . ."

"Stop!" I said sharply. "I have met you in a previous existence. You are going to say that a solitary Uhlan appeared sharply outlined against the sky behind M. Jules' farm." He nodded feebly.

"The red trousers had left the village half an hour before to look for the hated Prussian in the cafés of the neighbouring town. You were alone when the spiked helmets marched in. You can hear their shrieking fifes to this day." He wept quietly.

I went on. "There was an officer with them, a proud, ugly man with a butter-coloured moustache. He saw the little Mimi and drove his coarse Suabian hand upward through his Mecklenburger moustache. You dropped on one knee. . . ." But he had fled.

In the first of the three cafés I saw a second old man. "Come in, Monsieur," he said. I waited on the doorstep. "It was on just such an afternoon. . . ." I went on. At the other two cafés two further old men attempted me with the story; I told the last that he was rescued by Zouaves, and walked happily to the station, to read about Vichy Célestins until the train came in from the south.

The Russo-Japanese War is a more original subject and derives its particular flavour from the airy grace with which Sir Ian Hamilton has described it. Like this:

WAO-WAO, *Jan.* 31.—The *rafale* was purring like a *mistral* as I shaved this morning. I wonder where it is; must ask ——. —— is a charming fellow with the face of a Baluchi Kashgai; and a voice like a circular saw.

11.40.—It was eleven-forty when I looked at my watch. The shrapnel-bursts look like a plantation of powder-puffs suspended in the sky. Victor says there is a battle going on: capital chap Victor.

2 P.M.—Lunched with an American lady-doctor. How feminine the Americans can be.

7 P.M.—A great day. It was Donkelsdorp over again. Substitute the Tenth Army for the Traffordshires' baggage waggon, swell Honks Spruit into the roaring Wang-ho, elevate Oom Kop into the frowning scarp of Pyjiyama, and you have it. The Staff were obviously gratified when I told them about Donkelsdorp.

The Rooskis came over the crest-line in a huddle of massed battalions, and Gazeka was after them like a rat after a terrier. I knew that his horse-guns had no horses (a rule of the Japanese service to discourage unnecessary changing of ground), but his men bit the trails and dragged them up by their teeth. Slowly the Muscovites peeled off the steaming mountain and took the funicular down the other side.

I wonder what my friend Smuts would make of the Yentai coal mine? Well, well.—"*Something accomplished, something done.*"

The technical manner is more difficult of acquisition for the beginner, since it involves a knowledge of at least two European languages. It is a cardinal rule that all places should be described as *points d'appui,* the simple process of scouting looks far better as *Verschleierung,* and the adjective "strategical" may be used without any meaning in front of any noun.

But the military manner was revolutionized by the war. Mr. Belloc created a new Land and a new Water. We know now why the Persian commanders demanded "earth and water" on their entrance into a Greek town; it was the weekly demand of the Great General Staff, as it called for its favourite paper. Mr. Belloc has woven Baedeker and geometry into a new style: it is the last cry of historians' English, because one was invented by a German and the other by a Greek.

SOME STRATEGISTS

It must be nearly thirty years since the late Captain Mahan stood silent on a peak in Darien in the first shock of the discovery that the waters of the Atlantic and Pacific Oceans were wet. The thoughtful sailor indulged his companions of the United States Naval War College with the wild surmise that a liquid of this character might be expected to sustain the weight of warships and that the operation of such vessels would possess a distinct importance in determining the result of disputes between nations, always provided that they were not (as in the happy cases of Switzerland, Luxemburg, and Liechtenstein) entirely cut off from the sea. The leaping inferences of his discovery were communicated, through his English publisher, to the inhabited world, and the doctrine of Sea Power became (if it ever needed to become) a commonplace. Yet there was a real merit in Mahan's work. It is easy to complain of him, as Wilde complained of a contemporary, that he pursued the obvious with the enthusiasm of a shortsighted detective; but it is even easier to forget that he produced an articulate and comprehensible statement of matters which had not, before he wrote, been stated at all. Sea Power had been for several centuries the practice of the British Navy, and the British Navy, by reason of certain faults in its up-bringing and the difficulties of literary composition on a mobile surface, is not given to self-expression. Before the year 1880 there existed hardly a single statement of the broad principles of naval strategy, and even now there are extraordinarily few. Portsmouth has never produced the counterpart of those admirable, if unbound, little volumes of professional prose which French soldiers used to publish at Nancy; and since the *Grande muette* has declined to explain its fundamental principles, one is grateful to the enterprising American who undertook the work. There are no surprises in his revelation, and the air of discovery is sometimes a trifle irritating; the constant treatment of Venus as a new planet would damn any astronomer, and no one could bear many walks with a man who insisted regularly on striking across Primrose Hill as an undiscovered watershed.

But if Mahan discovered nothing in particular, he discovered it very well. One feels the need of his expository method whenever a large and obvious fact emerges into the area of military science without an adequate statement of its elements. That is precisely what has just occurred in the case of railways. We all know a railway when we see one, and we can all grasp, if we can read a newspaper, what railways mean in modern war. It is obvious beyond the faintest hope of novelty that European warfare, as it was practised on the French and Polish frontiers, was a struggle for railways conducted by men at the end of railways who would be reduced to fisticuffs in a week and to starvation in a fortnight if their railways could be paralyzed. But so far as broad and popular exposition in general terms is concerned, the military science of railways is a subject as uncharted as Lake Chad when our fathers went to school. It is a white patch on the map that cries out for the explanatory longitude, the illuminating platitude of the American sea-captain. Wanted, one cries, wanted a Mahan.

It was Mr. H. G. Wells who insisted, long before they took the horse omnibuses off the road, that the world would be transformed by its means of communication. The change was one of those queer, unconscious achievements of the Nineteenth Century, when little men in black coats produced the most astonishing results whilst thinking hard all the time about something else. It began in the year 1830,

26

when a British regiment was trundled thirty-four miles in two hours over the far from permanent way of the Liverpool and Manchester Railway. Then, like most things in the progress of Europe, having been done by an Englishman, it was explained by a German. A Westphalian bearing the honoured, if slightly misspelt, name of Harkort startled his Lantag with railway projects and produced a pamphlet on the military value of a line between Minden and Cologne. His heated imagination played recklessly round the prospect:

> Let us suppose that we had a railway and a telegraph line on the right bank of the Rhine from Mainz to Wesel. Any crossing of the Rhine by the French would then scarcely be possible, since we should be able to bring a strong defensive force on the spot before the attempt could be developed.
>
> These things may appear very strange today; yet in the womb of the future there slumbers the seed of great developments in railways, the results of which it is as yet quite beyond our powers to foresee.

It was the year 1833, and the German public was promptly informed by one distinguished soldier that infantry would arrive sooner if they marched, whilst another added that the conveyance of cavalry and artillery by train would be a sheer impossibility. Meanwhile the War Office produced in 1846 a "Regulation relative to the Conveyance of Her Majesty's

Forces, their Baggage and Stores, by Rail," and Belgium gave the Continent a lead in railway construction. The military advantages of a railway system were repeatedly emphasized in admirable prose by the subjects of Louis Philippe; and there was some interesting early work in Central Europe. The Prussians moved 12,000 men over two lines in 1846; a Russian army corps entrained in 1849 and moved into Austrian territory to suppress the revolution in Moravia; and the Austrians took 75,000 men, 8,000 horses, and 1,000 waggons from the Danube to the Silesian frontier in that movement of troops which resulted in the humiliation of Prussia at Olmütz and sixteen years of smouldering resentment that found expression at Königgrätz.

Railways entered the repertory of European warfare too late to be used by Napoleon or to be more than tried by von Moltke. With a single line from Paris to Vienna the Emperor might have conquered Europe in two months instead of in two years, and a railway system would have multiplied the *Grande Armée* to hold off the Russians in the Grand Duchy of Warsaw whilst the English in the Peninsula were driven into the sea. The first European war to be conducted after the construction of railways was the campaign of Magenta and Solferino. Napoleon III took a French army into Italy and, after making considerable use of the railway between Paris and various stations on the south coast and on the Italian frontier, he ignored its existence with heroic completeness in an attempt to conduct his operations on orthodox Napoleonic lines. Von Moltke's papers, in which the design against Austria was progressively developed in the years between 1860 and 1866, are a mine of various wisdom upon the political and military conformation of Europe; but there is no adequate treatment of railways. In the campaign of 1866, which saw the entry of the field telegraph, the Prussians made no brilliant use of their own and the Saxon systems, but there was a sensational employment of railways on the Italian frontier; the Austrian commanders were scandalized by the repeated appearance of hostile troops in numbers quite unrecognized by the rules, and a French military writer was inspired to lyrical comment on the subject in the *Spectateur Militaire* for September, 1869. Nine months later his country was invaded by the armies of the North German Confederation and its allies after an excellent concentration by railway in the Palatinate.

But the real impetus to the development and to the progress of so many branches of modern warfare came from the American Civil War. The earnest and irritable men who conducted the somewhat tangential operations of the Union armies were confronted by every problem of the military use of railways. The supply of troops by rail-borne commissariat, the destruction of railways (which has always been a distinctively American, though latterly an almost exclusively Mexican accomplishment), and the organization of railway services by technical troops all emerged from the long conflict. McCallum was the first of the railway soldiers, and the troubles of his subordinates with the military element are illustrated by an appealing telegram of the War Department:

Be patient as possible with the Generals. Some of them will trouble you more than they will the enemy.

Africa was introduced to the military railway by Lord Kitchener's conquest of the Soudan by rail; and in Asia the Trans-Siberian Railway was the instrument with which Russia conducted her astonishing defensive in Manchuria at the end of a single line.

The late war, which began with a German move along the ordinary route of the Paris-Berlin expresses and degenerated in eight weeks into a scramble for the railway junctions of Northern France, was conducted with railways, for railways. The

German defensive on the eastern front consisted
merely of movements round the parallel lines of the
German railway-citadel, and the offensive of 1915
was solely a lunge at the railway system of Poland.
Without railways the war would have ended in the
suburbs of Berlin in six weeks. It was the railway,
and the railway alone, that made possible the vast
and paralyzed armies that lay helplessly opposite to
each other across Europe, breathing heavily, eating
what their railways brought them, and shooting away
what their railways could carry of the national ac-
cumulations of metal goods.

It was in the Great War the hand that ruled the
railway rocked the world. There was no romance
in it. We have learnt in bitterness that the glory
of war is the wretchedness of its most broken man,
and the dignity of war is the vulgarity of its basest
recruiting-poster. The call of Mr. Kipling's red
gods dwindled to Mr. Tennant's sartorial enquiry
whether our best boy was in khaki; and as the young
men marched away, our ideals faded until we were
left alone with those less disinterested men of business in whose hearts Mr. Asquith's burning words will
always find an echo: "No price," as the contractor
said, "can be too high when honour and freedom are
at stake."

Warfare had been invested by Victorian romance

with a certain glamour. It was generally believed that the saviours of their country would leave for the railway-station in scenes of mild but appropriate emotion, returning after a short interval victorious and bronzed to the proper tint of brown, which is familiar to all playgoers as the unfailing indication of successful military service. But in the autumn of 1914 we were thrust suddenly into reality; it was an experience which the people of Europe are not likely to forget. In absolute silence and without a single aid to the heroic imagination men went into the first campaign of the European War. If they expected it to be autumn manœuvres with ball-cartridge, they were bitterly surprised. Moving with the secrecy of criminals, men killed one another with machines; at the orders of their Governments, which had for many years laboriously discouraged crime, they committed murder, burglary, and rape. The method of European warfare was exposed once and for all. It had been familiar to the Middle Ages as an aristocratic celebration of the harvest festival, and it had been permitted to survive in modern times as a form of international argument, as the ultimate form of controversy in the European family: a nation went to war when its foreign relations became impossible. In the area of actual warfare it varied between heroic mud-larking and the abomination of desolation; and outside in Europe it presented itself as an enormous and unfascinating blend of a bank failure and a railway accident. That is a European war.

SOME CRITICS

THE sensitive person, if he is still alive, must be having a most disturbing time. One fancies the poor gentleman, with his fine *flair* for consistency and his exact eye for an historical parallel, a trifle out of breath in the Revue of Revues in which it is our present privilege to live. Parties and principles join hands and whirl round him in a ragtime *Carmagnole;* and even the solemn processes of the Constitution, having once been set to the syncopated goose-step of the Defence of the Realm Regulations, can never be completely relied on again. Indeed, he resembles more than a little as he blinks his way across the contemporary stage, that "ancient, contemplative person" whose reminiscent bath-chair was trundled by Mr. Henry James through the stamp and thunder of *The American Scene.*

But of all his senses it is the hearing that has been most cruelly assaulted by the Saturnalia *de nos jours.* For the first months after the outbreak of war it

vibrated painfully to the chest-notes of our leading
thinkers on other subjects attuning themselves inde-
fatigably to the new European accompaniment. Then
for a short but harrowing period the national intelligence was at the mercy of any Boanerges that could
command a luncheon-club and a reporter. In a later
phase, as the war dropped to a deeper note and
enemy action checked the free import of paper-
making materials, his ears reverberated with the in-
vitations of the organ-voice of England to tuck in
his twopenny (or, as it has since become, his three-
penny). Followed a sound of breaking window-glass
and the voice of one Billing in the wilderness. And
so the shifting voices of the war passed painfully
through his hearing into history. It must have seemed
sometimes to the listener like the dreary study by a
sleepless man of the stages of sound which carry last
night into to-morrow, the gradual change from the
crowding and confidential voices of late evening to
the loud and scattered talkers of the first small hours
and from them to the quiet of the middle night, the
miscalculations of premature and inaccurate poultry,
the first light, and the earliest horse. With the great
dawn of the armistice he could hear the normal traffic
of the world passing his windows again, and the
hoofs of all the hacks in England began to rattle
noisily over the cobble-stones to the cheerful clatter

of Sir James Barrie's cans as he went round with
the milk of human kindness.

But before the reviving national voices had recovered their full strength they were interpenetrated
and almost drowned by a new note of a deeper and
more sinister pitch. The *cri du* coroner, which started
its unobtrusive undertone in the remoter corners of
the newspapers, swelled gradually fuller and louder
and deeper until at last, dominating every competing
voice, it rolled from shore to shore with the proud
resonance of an accompanist that has succeeded in
submerging the solo.

It is not so long since the late Lord Tennyson
warned his fellow-countrymen that kind hearts are
more than coroners, and it is hardly surprising that a
public which has always disregarded its poets appears recently to have enthroned its coroners at an
unprecedented altitude. Their *obiter dicta,* their
lightest ejaculations, their considerate announcements of forthcoming attractions secured for the next
sitting have been quoted with a volume of publicity
that must be unspeakably distasteful to those re-
ticent men. But persevering doggedly in face of
the discouragements offered by verbatim reports and
sketching in court, those *macabre* exponents of medi-
cal jurisprudence, whose surroundings combine the
attractions of an operating theatre with the fasci-

nation of the Third Degree, did and more than did
the duty which England expected of them. There
was an ugly rush of Daniels come to judgment, and
the Peace Conference was triumphantly elbowed into
those quiet corners of the paper in which the attention of sub-editors is alternately wooed by the disturbing progress of bee-disease in the Isle of Wight
and the gratifying longevity of maiden ladies in
Herefordshire. The public mind was completely
obsessed. Impressionable lovers shocked one another by writing that dope deferred maketh the heart
sick; and it is even said that a schoolboy, whose
passion for topicality had recently involved him in
serious trouble for translating *In hoc signo vinces,*
that fiery message of the firmament to the pious Emperor, by the still more startling sky-sign, "That's
the stuff to give them," was ordered to write twenty
cantos of Dante in a round hand as a penalty for
the suggestion that the gates of the Inferno were
superscribed "All dope abandon, ye who enter here."

The period was in every way a wearing one for
the national intelligence; but the worst of it has yet
to be described. A few months earlier the coroner
spirit, speaking with a slight but noticeable American
accent, had invaded the quiet chambers of literary
criticism, and the inquest was on Henry James. It
was conducted in a discreet periodical with an orange

cover by a number of distinguished members of our inmost *intelligentzia,* who maintained throughout the proceedings, which were somewhat painful, the perfect assurance of a *juge d'instruction* with a corpse up his sleeve. They were so thoroughly determined to "sit on" the body, as our dear author would have said, nudging us with his inimitably knowing inverted commas at the little colloquialism; and from certain passages in the summing-up they appeared to be inviting the jury to find that, in deference to the popular taste for excess in anæsthetics, the end had been due to æsthetics improperly administered.

There are great parts of Mr. Ezra Pound's roomy rather than voluminous *constatation* that, in his own austere phrase, "I must reject according to my lights as bad writing; another part is a specialité, a pleasure for certain temperaments only." One regrets that one cannot share it. There is a passage of delirious merriment about the *Notes on Novelists:*

The *Times* Literary Supplement had got so groggy that something had to be done. Orders went forth from Shushan wherein is the palace that "something had to be done." The "Lit. Sup." was on the blink; on the blink so shockin' an' staggerin' that something had to be done to boost up its giddy prestige. There were but two spotless paladins, two giddy Galahads available—Henry James and the impeccable Beerbohm. So Max and the great stylist were tackled, cajoled, bribed, wheedled, and what not. And the *Notes on*

SOME CRITICS

Novelists were "got out of the late Henry somehow, after all."

No.

Or, again, the following selection from the thoughts that rise in Mr. Pound on confrontation with one of the later novels:

The Awkward Age, fairy godmother and spotless lamb and all the rest of it. . . . Opening *tour de force*, a study in punks, a cheese *soufflé* of the leprous crust of society done to a turn and a niceness save when he puts on the *dulcissimo*, *vox humana*, stop. . . . These timbres and tonalities are his stronghold; he is ignorant of nearly everything else. It is all very well to say that modern life is largely made up of vellities, atmospheres, timbres, nuances, etc., but if people really spent as much time fussing, to the extent of the Jamesian fuss, about such normal, trifling, age-old affairs as slight inclinations to adultery, slight disinclinations to marry, to refrain from marrying, etc., etc., life would scarcely be worth the bother of keeping on with it. It is also contendable that one must depict such mush in order to abolish it.

This, with great respect—as one should say when one rises to interrupt a runaway coroner—is the merest literary jazz, with trap-drums banging, tin trays clashing, and the inspiriting ululations of all that splendid battery of sound producers with which the virility of the New World has enlivened the declining art of music.

But, apart from these distressing orchestral effects

39

and a somewhat disjointed series of staccato notes
which leave one with the misleading impression that
Mr. Pound's shirt-cuffs have been sent to the printer
instead of to the laundress, there is an admirable
residuum of hard, if somewhat loose-limbed, thinking.
The Little Reviewers have worked conscientiously
over the whole splendid ground; and one's only com-
plaint must be that, confronted with the body of an
author's completed works, they profess almost to a
man to see the deepest significance in the fragments:
it is a bad habit which they may have learnt from
some of our Grecians. And having in this manner
established their reputation as earnest scholars, they
proceed to maintain it by passing almost completely
over the humour of Henry James. There is that
splendid spoof account in *The American Scene* of
how the United States came to be started because
of the peculiar aptness of the fittings and fixtures
of a room in Philadelphia for some such occasion:

One fancies, under the high spring of the ceiling and before the great embrasured window-sashes of the principal
room, some clever man of the period, after a long look round,
taking the hint. "What an admirable place for a Declaration of something! What could one here—what couldn't
one really declare?" And then, after a moment: "I say, why
not our Independence?—capital thing always to declare, and
before any one gets in with anything tactless. You'll see
that the fortune of the place will be made."

40

Henry James initiating the American Revolution on grounds of pure upholstery is a magnificent picture, although one realizes how offensive it must be to Mr. Pound, who is continually anathematizing his "dam'd fuss about furniture." Indeed, it is a bias against the "minor mundanities," and the tendency to *"conspuer* . . . Henry James' concern with furniture, the Spoils of Poynton, connoisseurship, Mrs. Ward's tea-party atmosphere, the young Bostonian of the immature novels," that seems to have led these students into their gravest critical error. The work of the middle James in the years between 1889 and 1900 is dismissed with an intellectual curse as "this entoilment in the Yellow Book, short sentences, and the epigrammatic." It is a pity, because to another judgment it appears his best.

The work of Henry James has always seemed divisible by a simple dynastic arrangement into three reigns: James I, James II, and the Old Pretender. It is perhaps inevitable that the most bigoted Jacobites should cling closest to the Old Pretender; but whilst one applauds their loyalty, one can hardly defer to those critics who prefer the splendid rococo of the decadence to the rich purity of the prime. Strikingly small in number are the adherents of James I, a simple, cultured monarch ruling over a kingdom which must have consisted principally of the Atlantic Ocean, because it was bounded on the East by Paris and on the West by Back Bay. In the next reign the King handled his sceptre of language with a perfect control of his subjects and of the treatment which he royally accorded to them. With the discovery by James of the fatal art of dictation about the year of Queen Victoria's second Jubilee, he passed into history and the throne was claimed by the Old Pretender. He was the most engaging claimant that had ever planned a descent on England; but his career, as one reads it, was a long struggle to get back to something that he had somehow, somewhere lost. It was the art of his predecessors, the deft and gracious handling of English words for the rendering of transparent thought; and it is with something more than a desire to irritate Mr. Pound (and perhaps also Sir Edward Carson) that one may say that the greatest of the three was James II.

SOME AMBASSADORS

All nations get the ambassadors that they deserve. One seems to have heard something like this before. Indeed, it is the merit of such general truths that one always seems to have heard something like them before. At any rate one clings, with the patient obstinacy of a politician with a congenial platitude, to the introductory saw that all nations get the ambassadors they deserve. The distinguished gentlemen who serve them abroad in the high dignity of these elevated positions serve them right.

And yet it is not always easy to believe. Frequenters of palaces are sometimes startled by a strange disparity between the diplomats and the countries which they represent. One may test it on those summer evenings when the King of England holds his Court, and the charming ladies of the Associated Power ("Gigantic Daughters of the West," in Lord Tennyson's well-meant but infelicitous phrase) shorten the lives of hunted Second Secretaries with the necessary arrangements for their obeisance to an alien despot. Outside, by the pale light of a London sunset, obliging policemen with all their medals on dislocate the traffic in the Mall for the convenience of their sovereign's guests. Somewhere beyond, an exquisite company presses dynastic carpets behind the drawn blinds of the Palace—heads high (to keep their feathers straight), eyes front (to check the rising terror of scarlet liveries and knee-breeches aligned along their path). Gentlemen-ushers wave them on; and they go, like the brisk, determined lady in the little piece which Henry James wrote for Miss Ruth Draper (does she ever do it now?) "the full length of American woman's right"—to the steps of the British throne. There is a riot of precedence, an orgy of deportment. But the *clou* of the whole charade is the Diplomatic Circle. By far the most amusing guests at the Court are the ambassadors. These brightly tailored gentlemen are cast to play the parts of entire nations. They peer about politely above vivid explosions of gold lace, and represent large populations in foreign countries. That is when one begins to wonder whether all nations quite deserve the ambassadors that they get.

France, in this elegant game, is an amiable Count, who but rarely wears a cap of liberty. Spain is a slim gentleman with quite an intelligent interest in modern art. Italy, whom one might have expected to make his entry in a smother of black, symbolical haberdashery behind the pounding of drums of operatic reaction, really looks quite manageable. It is not always easy, as one looks round the Circle, to reconcile these figures with the parts which they have to play. Mild-eyed gentlemen in glasses represent fierce little populations; and stern, military figures embody rather oddly the sedate ideals of steady, commercial races. It was on this diplomatic scene, that the exacting part of those United States was played, for three long years, by Colonel George Harvey.

England, which is annually reminded upon the anniversary of Trafalgar that she expects that every man will do his duty, expects a great deal of the American Ambassador. Other diplomats are free to play their parts according to their tastes. Indeed, few people pay the slightest attention to their admirable performances. They open the right number of exhibitions of their national art; they advert, in appropriate language, to the peculiar ties (*liens indestructibles*) which have always united their country to Great Britain; they sit, with the requisite expression of gravity, in the Distinguished Strangers' Gallery of the House of Commons, when matters relating to their fatherland are under discussion. But no one really cares a bit.

How much more eminent is the destiny of their

American colleague. He plays his part on a higher and more lighted stage. This happy diplomat enjoys a strange prominence in the public view; and one is sometimes tempted to wonder, quite respectfully, why. Perhaps he owes it to the vivid contrast of his garish uniform with the modest gold lace of his official colleagues. The flamboyant blackness of that coat, the blinding iridescence of that evening shirt lend him a magnificence that is almost Oriental, as he crosses the subdued, the Quaker-like background of diplomatic life. He is bound to be noticed anywhere. Even the waiters, in such circles as ambassadors frequent, are dressed with a more modest gaudiness than he.

Another element combines to render him strangely conspicuous in the Diplomatic *corps*. His language, when he says something in public, can be understood. His hearers cheer, and even laugh, in the right places. He does not speak in that broken English, which is the language of diplomacy; and reporters are in a position to misrepresent him almost as though he were a native statesman. It is nothing that his idioms are misunderstood; it is less than nothing that the point of his raciest, most republican anecdote is always exquisitely missed. The proud fact remains that, while sub-editors relegate all foreign diplomats to the Court Circular, the American Ambassador is News—sometimes good News, and sometimes. . . .

It is a lofty calling; and young aspirants may be assumed to land at Liverpool with a high sense of its distinction. But, unhappily perhaps, convention rarely permits them to play the part according to their private tastes. Certain gestures are prescribed by ritual. There is a certain tradition, to which all performers are expected to conform; and their personal characteristics are submerged in the careful presentation of this conventional figure. The bright young actress who attempts to introduce new business into *Phèdre* at the Français meets with a sharp rebuff. So, one imagines, would any enterprising diplomat who was caught tampering with the traditional part of the American Ambassador to the Court of St. James's. But they never do.

This figure, proud result of a hundred years of peace and the long frontier where teeming populations . . . without a soldier or a gun . . . by the calm waters of gigantic Lakes . . . in amity side by side—this strange totem of Anglo-American friendship is expected, as his principal occupation, to make speches after dinner. He is expected to make them with fluency and rather wittily, and to follow certain recognized openings.

For the majority of his public utterances, he will find it sufficient to allude, in a semi-religious tone,

47

to the larger (that is to say, the more deceased)
figures of that literature which is shared (and equally
neglected) by his countrymen and King George's.
He will find that meaningless expression, "glorious
heritage," of infinite value. If the chairman mentions
Bunyan, the ambassador is expected to double and
play Milton. He may even, in moments of deep
emotion, touch on Shakespeare and Edmund Burke;
but, in general, it is undesirable that he should con-
fess awareness of any author subsequent in date to
the Declaration of Independence.

Speeches of this simple pattern will carry him a
good way towards success. But upon some occasions
he will change his note and tread, with grave delibera-
tion, upon his hearers' toes in the familiar character
of the Candid Friend. This type of speech enjoys
the wildest popularity in England, because it serves
to remind opinion that the American Ambassador
is no mere foreign diplomat. If he is rude enough
it becomes apparent to a delighted populace that he is,
he must surely be, a blood relation. That is where he
achieves his most cherished effects; and connoisseurs
compare ambassadors according to their handling
of this familiar gambit. At his best he treats it
with a simplicity, a bluntness, which are "delightfully American," as that term was understood in
London half a century ago. By such arts as these

the American Ambassador of the day ministers to that complete misunderstanding, which is the sole safeguard against war.

Mr. Harvey embarked on this strange calling with certain radical advantages. He had a lively wit. His oculist had taken steps to render him easily identifiable, in any company, with his great country. And he was without previous experience in diplomacy. The last recommendation appears to have become quite indispensable for all diplomatic appointments made between the British and American peoples. A vacancy sets the authorities wondering what bright, middle-aged lad can be given a start in a new career as British Ambassador at Washington or American Ambassador in London. It is a brave experiment. But perhaps a hundred years of peace have justified it: a real diplomatist would probably have started a war out of a strict sense of professional duty.

Little was known of Mr. Harvey when he landed. Literary men (a limited and penurious class, of no political significance) were inclined at first to attach a slightly sinister meaning to the strange fact that two out of the last three American Ambassadors had been publishers. But this was quickly recognized as a sly national repartee to the persistent unofficial embassies of English authors in America. If Eng-

land was habitually represented on the lecture-plat-
form by men who write books, it was felt to be only
fitting that the United States should be officially embodied in one of those more useful members of
society who positively sell them. So there was no
obstacle to success in Mr. Harvey's distinguished
calling. A corporation lawyer might, perhaps,
have been more strictly in accordance with tradition. But a publisher was well enough. And Mr.
Harvey was no ordinary publisher.

That was, perhaps, his foremost attraction. It
was felt from the first that Mr. Harvey was a little
out of the ordinary. That sprightly figure seemed
to afford a welcome interruption of the smooth procession of *personæ gratæ* who had passed from
steamer to banquet, from banquet to unveiling, from
unveiling to steamer, and so to a memorial tablet in
some London church. Not (be it understood) that
Mr. Harvey was unwelcome. His impressive *per-
sona* was quite sufficiently *grata*. But he so obviously was not one of those stately national figures
to whom Great Britain, in its patient way, had grown
accustomed. One can remember them so well—that
grave presence, which the Executive has got so
tired of seeing about Washington that it sends it to
London, the accumulated wisdom of those long years
spent out of active politics.

But Mr. Harvey hustled on to the English scene with quite a different air. Not his the startled, deprecatory blink of the sage, exhumed suddenly from the cool darkness of his long retirement and projected into the vivid glare of the diplomatic footlights. He had so manifestly been engaged in doing something up to the very moment of his appointment. Perhaps he was doing it still. That was always, for most Englishmen, the exciting thing about Mr. Harvey.

He seemed to come to us straight out of the mysterious heart of American politics. He was understood to have invented President Wilson. He was even credited with the still more creative work of making President Harding. Great Britain acquiesced respectfully in this remarkable record of prestidigitation and waited to see a fakir who could make banyan trees grow out of nothing and throw empty rope ladders in the air, from the empty tops of which Presidential candidates emerged full-grown. It was a pleasant thrill; and British opinion had the comforting feeling that his next invention would not, at any rate, be President of Great Britain.

That was the basis of our respect for him. We rather liked him, because he seemed to have a sense of humour. Our sense of tradition was pleasantly gratified by his sure handling of the familiar opening of the Candid Friend. He began it early, and with his foot on the loud pedal. But, unhappily, as he became more friendly, his candour seemed to diminish; and one began to hear a lurking fear that he really liked us. That, in an American Ambassador, would never do. A dawning affection for the British people would be as fatal to the correct performance of his part as the loss by a British Ambassador at Washington of his sense of a secret superiority. But Mr. Harvey managed to keep it under pretty well. His arrival was the customary breath of fresh air into the stifling atmosphere of an ancient civilization; and his departure was a graceful shaking of secular dust from progressive feet. It was a most conscientious performance of a traditional part.

But his real attraction was his mysterious flavor of American politics. Our knowledge of the world is strangely limited. England is full of men who confidently profess an intimate knowledge of all the politics of the Continent. Not a *Bloc* can fall to the ground in a foreign Chamber without the reasoned comment of some British expert. They know the Right from the Left and the Centre from the Left-Centre. They can place the conflicting parties at the appropriate points of the political compass, with the accuracy of a cricket captain setting his fielders. Catholic Socialists and Fruitarian Clericals hold no mysteries for them; and they are thoroughly at home in the parliamentary *coulisses* of every country, except one.

American politics strike them completely dumb. They have rarely mastered the difference between a Republican and a Democrat: the connotations of both those terms are bewilderingly similar to the European mind. And when they have once grasped the distinction, they are at sea again when those great parties obstinately decline to manœuvre as two solid units and insist instead upon having grave internal differences.

It results from this elementary ignorance that the stately course of public life in the United States is completely missed by the British mind. It sees, instead, a brisk succession of unrelated happenings. Strange things are cast up by the deep and return to it again. Vast Conventions seem to rock with incomprehensible slogans. Sudden tides submerge outstanding figures, whom we had just learned to regard as international landmarks; and the receding waters leave stranded on the beach queer forms, which transcend our limited knowledge of natural history.

From the occult depths of this strange sea, Mr. Harvey came to us; and we were vastly impressed. Locked in his breast, we felt, was all the secret knowledge of a dweller in that mysterious clime. He must know where Presidents came from; and why they came; and where they went to. He was probably aware of the hidden springs of party discord. He might even know what it was all about.

Great Britain reverently stared; and Mr. Harvey played his splendid part. Out of those depths he came to us; and to them, we felt with increasing awe, he would presently return. It was, for the simple subjects of King George, a great experience. We felt that we had seen Arthur: almost, we had seen Merlin. And as the ship, that carried him into the mist, faded out across the sea, we seemed to hear him still faintly crying: "From the great deep to the great deep I go."

SOME FRENCHMEN

IT was the discovery of Laurence Sterne in the year 1767 that they order this matter better in France. Since the throne of St. Louis was occupied at the moment by Louis XV, the remark was probably inapplicable to anything except furniture and dance-music. But the reverend gentleman having omitted to state to which of those absorbing branches of human activity his comment was addressed, it has been appropriated since his lamented death by the whole heavenly host of critics and applied by them to every achievement of the mind of man from a rational system of registering heavy luggage to the more laborious businesses of poetic drama and the manufacture of field artillery. The observation has become one of the most golden items in our national treasury of misquotations; and perhaps it may serve as a convenient summary of that general appreciation of French effort which became common in the United Kingdom after Lord Landsdowne had inaugurated the *Entente Cordiale* of 1904.

SUPERS AND SUPERMEN

For six centuries the Englishman had regarded his cross-Channel neighbours with that settled and gloomy disgust which is congenial to his simple nature. Their manufactures were usually designated as kickshaws; their diet was believed to consist exclusively of the lesser molluscs and reptilians; and they wore the most preposterous hats. It was never known for certain, but it was darkly whispered, that they killed foxes with the bullet rather than with the dog; and their language was apparently composed of what Mr. Kipling has elegantly described as *doodeladays*. But this genial view, which had held the field since the reign of Edward III, was exorcised in less than six months in the reign of Edward VII by a diplomatic arrangement relating to some fisheries off Newfoundland and some rookeries in North Africa. It was discovered in this country, as the Egyptian question disappeared from the contested area of international politics, that the Frenchman Had Points. He was observed, after all, to be a solid fellow with many of the Anglo-Saxon virtues. Mr. Imré Kiralfy gave an eloquent expression to the idea by making a nightmare in stucco out of a goodsyard in Shepherds Bush. The *Entente* found a suburb plaster and left it plaster of Paris; and the people of England began to learn French.

From such small beginnings the French movement in these islands grew to imposing proportions;
and when the outbreak of war found Great Britain
ranged alongside of France, British opinion was
prepared for a generous appreciation of its ally. The
organized endeavour of a Latin race became the
model of English statesmanship; and to the profound
surprise of some of us, who had been preaching it
in partibus infidelium for a decade, the recovery of
Alsace-Lorraine was promoted to be an object of
national anxiety. The loyalty of the *Tailor and Cut-
ter* to its allies survived the yachting-cap which M.
Poincaré wore with knickerbockers during a mem-
orable visit to the Western Front; and the superiority of the French artillery, which one had suspected when Bombardier Wells succumbed to
Carpentier in the weeks preceding the war, became
a commonplace of military criticism. In fine, France
and all her works were very properly received with
a strong and sudden gust of acclamation, which would
inevitably remind Mr. Chesterton of nothing so much
as trumpets. This revolution was even more sweeping than that introduced about the same time in
artistic perspective by M. Mestrovic, when that eminent Serb, adopting the somewhat colloquial interpretation of a bust as being something which from all
appearances has burst, provoked the more conserva-

tive elements in English criticism to express a fervent hope that Britons never will be Slavs.

This temper of appreciation of France was, like all belated praise, somewhat uncritical; its compliments were all sincere and nearly all deserved, but it was sometimes a trifle undiscerning. France is (and had been before the fact was noticed in the London newspapers) the most civilized country in Europe. If the intelligent man of any period wished to know what Europe would be like in fifty years' time, he had only to look at the France of his day. But it is, perhaps, a misfortune that one had to go to war with the Germans in order to discover a platitude about the French.

By a stroke of delicious irony Mr. Kipling also was among the prophets. It is a fact of almost international significance that the high-priest of the Anglo-Saxon race brought himself to swing a censer before the Goddess of Reason, and it should be said for praise that he swung it very gracefully. Mr. Kipling, who had risen to a position of more than laureated eminence by the possession of an Imperial Eye and the use of the word "gadgets," discovered the French. It should be said, in fairness to that intelligent people, that it is some considerable time since the French discovered Mr. Kipling. His notes on the French Army were put together in a pamphlet,

and his skilled observation combined with an exact
and bitter appreciation of the nature of war to produce something more and better than mere war-
correspondence. It is characteristic that his chief
regret during a visit to the Western Front was an
ignorance of French slang, which debarred him from
any grasp of current military "shop." Mr. Kipling
has always counted among his gifts a genius for admiration. Sometimes he has admired things that are
not admirable; but when this power was directed,
as in the present case, upon a worthy object, the result was entirely satisfactory. The French people
at war was admired in a manner in which Mr.
Belloc, if he had not been otherwise engaged, might
have admired it:

> It is a people possessed of the precedent and tradition of
> war for existence, accustomed to hard living and hard la-
> bour, sanely economical by temperament, logical by training,
> and illumined and transfigured by their resolve and endur-
> ance.

That is a tone of self-respecting friendship which
is infinitely preferable to the rather shrill invective
with which the contemporary Mr. Kipling excoriated
the Hun. Talk about "animals" and "the Beast"
reminded one inevitably that no military damage is
done by "killing Kruger with your mouth." His
visit to the Vosges was crowded with the detail of

mountain warfare; and he drew with a loving and familiar pen "the same observation-post, table-map, observer, and telephonist; the same always-hidden, always-ready guns; and the same vexed foreshore of trenches, smoking and shaking, from Switzerland to the sea." But his generous appreciation of the French was marred by one singular error. Mr. Kipling reconciled his present praise with his past neglect of the French by a rather questionable theory that the war changed their psychology; and in order to emphasize this transformation he exaggerated their ruthlessness, until he has almost come to credit his allies with the worst qualities of their enemy. It is ungracious, when he is portraying Marianne, merely to hold the mirror up to Nietzsche; and it is almost disloyal, when he is describing the French temper, to talk Boche.

The true temper of the French is more easily discoverable in a view of the whole record of France than in a sketch, however expert and however intimate, of the French trenches. The Third Republic at war was an inspiring spectacle of logical and organized democracy, but the explanation of its qualities is to be sought rather in the past than in the present. The tone of the French armies was derived less from the foundling constitution of 1875, which history has fathered upon M. Wallon, than from the great days of the Monarchy, the First Republic, and the First Empire. That tone has been tempered by France's loss of her illusions. There was no appetite in those days of effort for *gloire,* the gadfly of all mad policies, because it had been discovered in 1815 that armies which marched into Berlin and Moscow and Vienna merely provoke other armies to march into Lille and Nancy and Paris. There is little taste for Cæsarism and hero-worship, because, as M. Hanotaux has written, France is cured of individuals and Utopias. The French are a modern people; and the spectacle of a modern people at war is only less splendid than the spectacle of a modern people at peace. But the more modern a people is, the more closely and clearly does it derive from its ancestors. That is why the study of French history is essential to any man who wishes to understand French politics.

The English, who are rarely diffident in writing upon their neighbours, have attempted with singular rarity to write the story of France. The First Empire, of whose *bric-à-brac* they are passionate collectors, has produced nothing among them beyond a mediocre biography; and the remainder of French history has been treated as a somewhat barren field peopled only by the Scottish Jacobins of Thomas Carlyle and several historical characters of sinister appearance impersonated by the late Sir Henry Irving. It is unfortunate; because just as the history of Italy is the history of European art and the history of England is the history of European expansion, so the history of France is in the fullest sense the history of European policy. Every movement which has resulted in the transformation of European states has radiated from or converged upon the city of Paris; even a British diplomat knows French.

The French line from Arras to the Alsatian pine-trees was a long scroll upon which the whole of French history was written. There was the thrifty statecraft which had added one field to another until the lord of Paris became the King of France; the slow effort of the lunge which drove the French frontier nearer and nearer to the Rhine; and the splendid makeshifts, as Victor Hugo called them, of the Revolution, which swept the kings over the border and the flag of the Republic after them. France is no novice at the game of European war; it is a long story, which begins in anthropology and ends with the White Paper of Sir Edward Grey.

There was once a British historian of the French whose facts were accurate and well-arranged, his military (and especially his Napoleonic) history intelligible, and his manner as detached as a proletarian shirt-cuff. But he succumbed to an astonishing assertion about the Frenchman's "lack of historical sense," in a country where every candidate for Parliament can talk for days about the *principes de* 1789, and will on the smallest provocation describe his adversary as a *patriote An II.* or a *vielle barbe de* 1848. One can hardly imagine an Englishman taunting a reactionary with the fate of Monmouth's army at Sedgemoor; but the French democrat will tell him about the *armée de Condé* as soon as look at him. One might as well rebuke an Ulsterman for his ignorance of the public career of William III.

A more serious fault in the average French history is that it generally ends in the year 1871. After an admirably balanced narrative, in which one sees the characters of the present scene assembling in the wings, the historian rings down the curtain at the Treaty of Frankfort. Now the history of France, unlike the *History of France,* does not leave off in 1871. *Vixere fortes post Agamemnona,* as Horace almost said. Although the public appearances of M. Grévy were less impressive than the epiphany of Napoleon, the Third Republic is far more important to all of us than the First Empire. To leave one's knowledge of France with the provisional Presidency of M. Thiers is to produce a completely false impression. It may be unattractive for the historian to descend from the windy heights of Napoleonic diplomacy to the *mares stagnantes* of Parliamentary history. There is something unheroic about the *dictature de M. Joseph Prudhomme;* and politicians with the appearance of head-waiters are dull company, even if they speak with the tongues of angels. Yet it remains true that our late Allies were not lit on their way to war by the blazing torches of the Revolution or the flaring gas-jets of the Second Empire; but they chose their path with foresight and they walked it with caution under the mild light of the *République athénienne.* The history of the Third Republic is the last and most vital chapter in the history of France. The curious thing about history is that it really happened: some of it is happening now.

SOME MORE FRENCHMEN

An Englishman is a man who lives on an island in the North Sea governed by Scotsmen: that is why it is called self-governing. His occupations are simple, but absorbing. In the intervals of earning money he practises (or preaches) the family virtues, reads (for the duration of the war) twenty-five newspapers in the week, and regards his weather, his relations, and his Government with a settled disgust. As the result, possibly, of an indifferent climate he is a person of somewhat slow perception. With regard to persons of importance he makes it a rule never to notice them until they are dead; and with regard to countries his practice is, thanks to his classical education, much the same.

Thus in the Eighteenth Century any gentleman could tell you all about the Greek Republics and the Roman Empire, but nobody in England, except Edmund Burke and the Earl of Chatham, was aware of the existence of its thirteen North American colonies, until they very pardonably revolted in order to remind the Englishman that they were still where he had put them. He had not noticed in the Nineteenth Century that he possessed a considerable Empire overseas, until the fact was discovered for him by Lord Beaconsfield and emphasized by Mr. Chamberlain. And, so recently as August, 1914, he made the startling discovery that he lived next door to Europe. It may be that, as we discovered the British Empire in the last century, so in the Twentieth Century we shall discover Europe. In this age of science all things are possible.

To the Englishman his island is a piece of land entirely surrounded by foreigners. The majority of these people are believed to live in a continent lying off the mouth of the Thames and known as Europe. Certain parts of it, as, for example, the Swiss mountains, the French Riviera, and the Italian picture galleries, are reserved for the holidays of Englishmen; but the remainder is entirely given up to foreigners. These foreigners, it has been observed by Englishmen who have ventured among them, differ in degree but not in kind. They are marked in every instance by an obstinate refusal to converse in English. This unreasonable objection compels the Englishman to toy lightly (or painfully) with the various absurd languages which they use among themselves.

SOME MORE FRENCHMEN

Before the war the Englishman recognized several distinct species of foreigners. There were the Germans, a peaceful people devoted to music, philosophy, and wood carving, who were reported recently to have directed their energies into the path of commerce; these could be distinguished by an inability to pronounce the letter "w" and the universal wearing of spectacles. Then there was the dark-haired foreigner of the Mediterranean. If he was playing the guitar, fighting bulls, or asleep, you knew him for a Spaniard; but if he divided his time between the tenor parts in opera and the precarious art of eating macaroni, he was an Italian. Then there was the Russian, whom you could always tell by his knout, his fur hat, and the cigar-cases which were apparently attached to the outside of his clothes. But, above all, there was the Frenchman, who was the foreigner *par excellence.*

Five centuries of Anglo-French hostility had gone to the making of our imaginary Frenchman, before the Lansdowne Convention of 1904 ended him once and for all. He was a magnificent creature. Because in the Eighteenth Century beef-eating England fought France for the control of India and North America and noticed that its enemy was a trifle unorthodox in his *hors d'œuvres,* we were all brought up to believe that Frenchmen lived exclusively upon frogs. And because at the end of that century France crusaded against Europe in the high name of the French Revolution, every Englishman was given to understand that every Frenchman was a gesticulating jackanapes with a farcical falsetto.

The generation of the late Prince Albert regarded the generation of Napoleon III as a shocking blend of Popery and the gay life; and because the sporting England of Queen Victoria could never understand the unathletic France of President Thiers, we have all in our time conjured up delightful visions of legions of little Frenchmen in flat-brimmed silk hats going fox-shooting with packs of poodles. No picture of life in Calais was too ludicrous to be believed in Dover; that is one of the advantages of being an Island Race.

It is almost impossible to analyze the causes of such national mistakes; when a whole race goes wrong, it is not simple to find the first blunder. After all, nobody ever did understand his neighbours; one misinterprets the proceedings of the man next door simply because he is the man next door.

England was at fault in its reading of France, because from 1360 until 1904 it regarded France with the eyes of an enemy. This hostility was interrupted by an interval in the reign of Elizabeth, a second interval in the reign of Charles II, and a third interval under the government of Walpole. But in the main it is true to say that England and France had been enemies from the reign of Edward III to the reign of Edward VII. There were periods when the exigencies of foreign policy dictated an *entente,* and diplomacy did its best to unite the two countries; but it was a friendship of governments, and the individual Englishman was never the friend of the individual Frenchman. Now you never understand your enemy: possibly that is why he is your enemy.

But it must not be thought that England alone was guilty of errors of this type. France in its time has misread England almost as completely as England has misread France. It is probably untrue that on this island we travel through a darkness of perpetual fogs to buy our wives by public auction at Smithfield. But until ten years ago these stimulating facts as to our climate and habits were articles of faith with Frenchmen of intelligence; that is the French error about England. It was equally untrue that France had lived for the past forty years so entirely in the nightmare memory of the *Année Terrible* that French politicians would resent no insult and French soldiers could resist no onset; that was the German error about France.

The British error about France came from two causes: a failure to appreciate the truth about French history and an inability to observe the truth about the France that is living under our eyes. When British opinion is set right about the past of France, it will be in a position to see straight about its present. But until it can get both of these things into a true perspective, it will continue to make itself ridiculous whenever it thinks of a Frenchman.

The first fallacy about the French is that they are frivolous. This illusion takes two forms, each of which is extremely popular in England: a belief that the French are light-headed in their public life and light-minded in their private life. Now the whole error with regard to French politics is probably derived from a misreading of the French Revolution. That group of events, which is generally believed to have consisted of an impulsive attack upon the Bastille, followed by an orgy of promiscuous decapitation, was in reality a solemn and progressive movement by which the society and government of France were reconstructed from top to bottom. It resulted from the accident that the reformers began at the top that they were compelled to cut off heads; but the Revolution itself was an effort of the whole population, directed by men of the professional class, against a discredited system of government and aristocratic privilege. The solemnity of the Revolution was consistent with the complete seriousness of the nation which had produced the Huguenots and was yet to produce the Third Republic.

The Third Republic, by which France has been governed since 1870, is the most serious government in Europe. It is no evidence of light-mindedness that Frenchmen have occasionally demonstrated their sincere preference for the republican form of government by dying for it on barricades. There is nothing flippant about street-fighting; and Tennyson was never farther from intelligence than when he delighted the subjects of Queen Victoria by a reference to "The red fool-fury of the Seine." It is true that in the beginning and middle of the last century Frenchmen showed a general uncertainty as to the precise form of government which they proposed to retain. But for fifty years they have retained the Republic.

The French Republic has no meretricious attractions. Its army has no dress uniform except the uniform in which it fights; its waiters (and even its head-waiters) wear the same clothes as its politicians (and even its President); and the *corps d'élite,* which had been the military pride of the Second Empire, were abolished in the first military reorganization of the Republic. France, which the good Englishman believes to live perpetual French farces as it revolves riotously round "Gay Paree," is the most serious

country west of China. Its Trade Unionism is fifty
years ahead of the rest of Europe; its inventors
showed us the way to the motor-car, the aeroplane,
and the submarine; and its genius is for the organization of peace. But its army was the most modern
and the most silent fighting force on the Continent.
One found in the little fortress-towns of Eastern
France little taste for the old shows of war. In the
streets every man was a soldier, because one had to
have soldiers; and in the country every hill top was
a gun-platform, because one had to have guns. That
is the military temper of modern France: it does not
set much store by glory, and it has changed so much
since its armies swept light-heartedly out into Europe
on the first wave of the Revolution. Because France
is civilized and because it is rich, France is a peaceful
country, and when a country fights for peace it makes
war with a hope that wins battles.

Modern France is neither a drill-ground nor a
play-ground. It is a great economic State alive with
the enterprise which has built up the industries of its
north and the agriculture of its centre, veined closely
with lines of railway and canal, and playing a leading part in the commercial life of Europe. That is
the France which Englishmen discovered with a shock
of surprise in the hot weather of 1914. It is a discovery which will affect more than a single war or a

single generation, because geography has made the co-operation of England and France in Western Europe as natural and inevitable as the co-operation of Germany and Austria in Central Europe. The discovery of France was something more than a discovery of an ally against Germany; it was the discovery of a neighbour whom England had not known for six centuries and by whom England will live in an exchange of all that is most valuable in both countries for more than the time of any man now living.

SOME ZIONISTS

NATIONALISTS, like most lovers and all idealists, are apt to be a trifle ridiculous in public. There is something about a political grand passion that seems to suspend a man, like the Prophet's coffin, somewhere between the sublime and the ridiculous, and there is in most cases no help for it. One must resign oneself to the splendid absurdity of the devotee. Romeo on the balcony, Mrs. Micawber reiterating her refusal ever to desert her husband, Robert Bruce's ill-timed passion for entomology, and Garibaldi freeing Italy in a four-wheeler, all fall, if one tilts the picture ever so little, into the faintly ludicrous attitude of persons in the grip of strong emotions. Any nationalist, whether the object of his affections is Achill Island or the Banat of Temesvar, is subject to this engaging failing. He is, like that impersonator of Hamlet (now, alas! no more), who could be funny without being vulgar, most entertaining when his endeavour is to be most impressive.

But in all the rollicking, carnival procession of

Donnybrook nationalists, frankly farcical irreden-
tists, and patriots *pour rire,* there is one grim and
sad-coloured exception. A single national movement
of our time is insusceptible of entertainment, from
whatever angle of wit or malice it may be regarded;
even the peerless lance of Mr. Max Beerbohm once
splintered and broke against its sombre armour. The
patriotism of the Jew—that pitiable affection which
has no loved land to gaze at—is an utterly solemn
thing. Perhaps it is so because it is so old that, like
a traditional funny story, it has ceased to be funny;
or perhaps because by the queer accident of Jewish
history it happens to be a sacred as well as a national
thing. But, from whatever cause, it remains true that
the Parliament at College Green, the ever Greater
Serbia, and M. Paderewski's Polish *concerto* may
be full of humorous possibility; whilst no man will
dare to smile on the grey day when the long line of
bowed heads and stooping shoulders shuffles wearily
out of the little towns of Eastern Europe, and winds
slowly southward until the leaders look up and see
the sun over the land of their promise and their de-
liverance.

Zionism, is one may use the term for a moment
without begging any controversial question, is one
of the few just and sacred causes which the war, like
an absent-minded earthquake, has moved forward in-

advertently towards their splendid goal. Any narration of its evolution is the historical study of an idea. The material side of the movement has always seemed a matter of the profoundest indifference. Statistics of school attendance, of the export of Jewish-grown olives from Palestine, and of the number of gallons of water passed annually through the restored system of irrigation are bound to cut such a pathetic figure next to the splendour of the national ideal which is expressed in them. Frankly, one is depressed rather than impressed by information of this type, and it is an infinite relief to escape from that obtrusion of it which is so dispiriting a feature of most national publications.

Patriots rarely excel in the composition of reliable prospectuses; and it should be realized that the strength of nationalists lies in the legitimate exercise of the imagination in the sphere of eloquence, prophecy, and the less austere forms of poetry, but that as map-makers, mineralogists, and compilers of racial statistics they tend to be beneath contempt. Their geese are all, as Henry James must have written somewhere, so quite magnificently swans that as bird-fanciers they are more than a little misleading. Indeed, there is a wistful Mexican in one of Mr. Leacock's stories whose *cri du cœur* might have been borrowed by almost any of the "nations struggling to be free," whose energetic delegates picketed the revolving doors of the Hotel Majestic. "Alas, my poor Mexico," he exclaimed, "she wants nothing but water to make her the most fertile country of the globe! Water and soil, these only, and she would excel all others. Give her but water, soil, light, heat, capital, and labour, and what could she not be!" That is an entirely legitimate travesty of what one fears to find on opening any study of Zionism by any leading Zionist. The material side of the movement is as unimportant to most of us as the pigments of a great picture or the geology of the Parthenon frieze. All that matters is the fact of the movement itself, and the slow but gathering momentum with which it moves.

The theme of a great part of the story should have a peculiar fascination for Englishmen. Without minimizing unduly the effort of foreign communities and the sympathy of Continental thinkers, it seems to show that the government of England has played a full and gracious part in the first and last scenes of the long tragedy of the Wandering Jew. Two and a half centuries ago the Lord Protector in Council reversed the Act of Edward I and readmitted the Jews to the territory of the English Republic. This response of Puritan opinion to the Jewish appeal was not surprising, because at no other time have the

English, or indeed any other European community, been more pre-eminently a people of the Book. A government whose heavy cavalry owed its victories to the inspiration of Joshua almost more than to the tactics of Gustavus Adolphus could hardly have made any other decision. But the present interest of it lies in the queer Zionist significance of the petition of Manasseh Ben-Israel and David Abrabanel. It was their belief that the return to Palestine would not be possible until the world-wide scattering of the race was complete. The return to the western islands was regarded as the final consummation of the Diaspora: "Let them enter England and the other end would be reached." So the last place of exile was to be the first station of the long homeward journey; and it was made possible by the Bible Christianity of the Commonwealth of England. And the last chapter of the same story was written when in the same capital city of Western Europe and in the closing months of a European war His Majesty's Government gave formal British recognition to the Jewish effort, speaking through Lord Robert Cecil, in an utterance which would perhaps have startled the Elizabethan Lord Burleigh considerably less than it would have scandalized the Victorian Lord Salisbury.

It is impossible to summarize the story of three centuries of Jewish and European opinion. The record of Zionism is a queer procession of widely different figures, all starting from far separated points and each at last converging into the great stream that drives south and eastward across the world towards the Holy Places. On the Jewish side one sees the slow drift that aligned the spasmodic romanticism of Disraeli with the patient effort of Sir Moses Montefiore and the faith and works of Pinsker, Hirsch, Herzl, Wolffsohn, Weizmann, and the rest; whilst the movement reacted on Europe in such odd forms as the Voltairean liberalism of Napoleon and his *Grand Sanhédrin,* Byron's facile and dilettante Semitism, and the urbane offer by Lord Lansdowne of a half-way house in East Africa, upon which the Foreign Office draftsman was amiably prepared to confer "a free hand in regard to municipal legislation and to the management of religious and purely domestic matters."

The Foreign Office has learnt several lessons since those quiet afternoons in 1903, and one of them stands out very clearly from the note which Mr. Balfour once contributed to a book on Zionism. His argument of one part of the Zionist case is a thoroughly skilful and attractive piece of writing. The average preface of the average statesman is a pitiable performance, because it is so apt to be written in a loud recitative with appropriate pauses for cheers and laughter. Mr. Balfour's conversational manner has a more level tone; and one tends to forget in the easy flow of his talk that one is hearing one of His Majesty's Principal Secretaries of State upon a question of high British policy. He faces frankly the deficiencies of the Jewish make-up:—

It is no doubt true that in large parts of Europe their loyalty to the State in which they dwell is (to put it mildly) feeble, compared with their loyalty to their religion and their race. How, indeed, could it be otherwise? In none of the regions of which I speak have they been given the advantage of equal citizenship, in some they have been given no right of citizenship at all. . . . It may well be true that when they have been compelled to live among their neighbours as if these were their enemies, they have often obtained, and sometimes deserved, the reputation of being undesirable citizens. Nor is this surprising. If you oblige many men to be money-lenders, some will assuredly be usurers. If you treat an important section of the community as outcasts, they will hardly shine as patriots.

He puts with eloquence the essence of the Zionist case:—

In no other case are the believers in one of the greatest religions of the world to be found (speaking broadly) among the members of a single small people . . . in the case of no other religion are its aspirations and hopes expressed in language and imagery so utterly dependent for their meaning on the conviction that only from this one land, only through this one history, only by this one people is full religious knowledge to spread through all the world.

And with something of the old dexterity which whitened the hair and shortened the lives of the early Tariff Reformers he eludes the point presented at his breast by the anti-Zionist opposition, by those "who, though Jews by descent, and often by religion, desire wholly to identify themselves with the life of the country wherein they have made their home. . . . They fear that it will adversely affect their position in the country of their adoption. . . . I cannot share their fears."

The objection is one that might have been answered in a deeper tone. The fortunate group that is in a position to raise it is the smallest portion of a suffering race; and it might well be retorted upon them that if by making a few hundred more aliens in London we can purchase a few thousand less graves in Poland, the price is not too large. For in the last resort, if the highest argument for Zionism is to be found in the prophet Isaiah, the case for it on the narrowest grounds is—Kishineff.

SOME GERMANS

WAR, in the considered judgment of the late General Sherman, is Hell. The comparison, although it begs an exciting question of teleology, is vivid and, it would seem, just. There are the outcries and the fire and even, in those countries which enjoy the blessings of Parliamentary institutions, the worm. But it is nowhere suggested, either in sacred or profane revelation, that the damned are provided with appropriate reading matter. Now when a miscalculation of the Great General Staff as to the train service between Liège and Paris sentenced the continent of Europe to a trial by ordeal, there was added to the physical torture of war the intellectual torture of books about it. Soldiers, sailors, travellers, and even dons and governesses hastened to adapt the peaceful art of stenography to the grim uses of war, and brought it, as they say, home to those suffering noncombatants who were physically unfit to run, but were unfortunately still able to read. Literary men did their Bit with the mechanical regularity of a child saying its Piece; and the cockpit of Europe re-echoed with the sound of innumerable writers murmuring contentedly, "Kiss me, Bernhardi: at least I have done my duty."

Other wars had seemed tolerable to the belligerents, because they were happily ignorant as to what they were fighting about. In those days it was satisfying to die for those princes of Europe who were said by a philosopher to "amuse their own leisure and exercise the courage of their subjects in the practice of the military art." But a war of ideas is about as entertaining as a drama of ideas. It is unnatural to expect a man to enjoy fighting with a carillon of explanation ringing in his ears and indicating precisely why, how, where, and with whom he is desired to contend. One is not stimulated to fight with beasts at Ephesus by the gift of a Natural History and a short guide to the neighbourhood; and it was even less reasonable to expect a footman to turn into a foot-soldier because he had read three Lives of Frederick the Great, *The Love Letters of Helmuth von Moltke,* and a colour book about Potsdam. It was perfectly proper that the people of England should acquire elementary information on the subject of Germany, whether they were fighting it or not; but it was a trifle undignified to make a European war the excuse for a gigantic course of University Extension.

One is unwilling to believe that the Roman parent in the Punic Wars was asked to purchase *The Confessions of Hasdrubal,* or *Hamilcar and the Women He Loved;* and it was improbable that *The Real Joan of Arc* would have found an extensive sale among the bewildered subjects of Henry VI. When Xenophon walked from Baghdad to the Black Sea, no Athenian bookseller issued *The First Ten Thousand;* and whilst Garibaldi was conquering Calabria in a four-wheeler, the Neapolitans were undisturbed by works upon Lord Brougham and his contributions to contemporary traction. But in the past five years these things have been paralleled and multiplied beyond measure, until the war is almost invisible under its own bibliography. The frightfulness of General von Bissing was as nothing to that of the average English book about his country. The catalogue of German wars has been written down in a manner that recalls the irreverent comment of Gibbon upon one of his authorities: "The coarse and undistinguishing pencil of Ammianus had delineated his bloody figures with tedious and disgusting accuracy." One may well regret, now that the autumn of our publishing season has deepened into the winter of our discontent, that so many persons should have so little to say about Prussia beyond what is either trite or Treitschke.

Literary critics have sometimes attempted to derive comfort from the saying of Lewis Carroll that "the number of lunatic books is as finite as the number of lunatics"; and it would be consoling if one could believe that the supply of books on Prussia is commensurate with the rapidly diminishing supply of Prussians. But in default of this happy arrangement, and failing a rational censorship of all matter calculated to amuse the enemy, our only hope seems to rest in the production of a definitive work which shall exhaust the subject without exhausting its readers. From this point of view the University of Oxford, which combines the study of history with the practice of politics, appears to have done all that is required of it. Two of the most popular lecturers in the School of Modern History, whose collaboration was a pleasing symptom of the party truce, produced a book which queered once and for all the Prussian pitch. There is no excuse, after the combined labours of Messrs. Marriott and Grant Robertson, for a continuance of the Saturnalia of dancing nonsense that has reeled round the makers of Prussia, since the finished article committed the supreme indiscretion of taking the first line of the chorus of the Jingo song literally. One cannot read this quiet and creditable piece of academic history and turn back again to the inaccurate melodrama of its competitors. The Prussian tradition was not strikingly interesting or (to the foreigner) particularly inspiring; but it was, for what that is worth, the tradition of the enemy. It is at least true to say that the last war is almost the first of English wars in which it has been safe for Englishmen to study the other side. If the subjects of George III had known as much about the French Revolution as the subjects of George V have lately learnt about Prussia, the Great War would have come to an unfortunate and sudden end in the hard winter of 1794.

The successive phases of Prussian history have grown to be almost painfully familiar. One begins with an acid comment on the indifferent and unlovely quality of the North German plain; and one is apt to forget, as that blasted heath comes to appear the natural haunt of the witches of military brutality and political craft, that Niccolo Macchiavelli enjoyed the amenities of the Arno. In any case European issues are not decided by questions of subsoil and top-dressing; and it may be that the unfriendliness of Nature has supplied Prussia with that mass of stubborn yokels which was the chief reservoir of its man-power. One passes direct by a pardonable transition, which omits the mosaic of mediæval Germany, to the age of

Frederick the Great; and one castigates with appropriate severity his Silesian and Polish transactions. It is usual to fix the making of Prussia in this eventful reign and by a pleasing symmetry to juxtapose the *incipium Borussiæ* with the *finis Poloniæ*. The Nineteenth Century of Prussian history is more varied. One opens with the collapse and resurrection of the kingdom in face of the French between the battle of Jena and the battle of Leipzig, and before the inexplicable coma of Prussia in the years between 1815 and 1848. One is then at liberty to study at full length the Prussianization of Germany by war, *Zollverein,* and treaty. That process is probably the most significant fact in modern Germany, which is now, as the Emperor William I remarked, "an extended Prussia." But it was preceded by a process which is of almost equal importance, but is commonly treated with absolute neglect. The Prussianization of Germany was merely the inevitable consequence of the Prussianization of Prussia; and that process was the work of a forgotten king, who has earned a seat among the Tartaric "Thrones, Dominations, Princedoms, Virtues, Powers" of the Prussian hierarchy from which neither Frederick nor Bismarck nor General von Bernhardi himself should displace him. Frederick William I, from whose singularly empty head Prussia sprang fully armed, has hardly made that noise in the world which he deserves. It is significant that even so careful a study as that of Messrs. Marriott and Grant Robertson devotes fifty pages to the achievement of Frederick the Great and barely ten to the work of Frederick William, which alone made it possible. Although Mr. Marriott (or Mr. Grant Robertson) admits that his reign was "the period in which all the most unlovely and forbidding qualities of Prussianism were scourged into the kingdom," Mr. Grant Robertson (or Mr. Marriott) is permitted to remark that "two such kings as Frederick William I, and Prussia would have ceased to contribute to the world anything but the ethics of Bridewell and the lessons of the guard-room": the comment recalls the writings of Macaulay alike by its eloquence and by its inaccuracy. The fascination of invective has tempted too many writers to forget that Frederick William made Prussia. He was followed by Frederick the Great as inevitably as Philip of Macedon was followed by Alexander. As Philip created the phalanx, so Frederick William created the Prussian infantry. His collection of giant grenadiers expressed a grotesque taste for human *bric-à-brac,* and his *grands soldats de parade avec leurs petits habits bleus et leurs cheveux poudrés à blanc* entertained his contemporaries; but they failed singularly to amuse the next generation in the

course of the Seven Years' War. He created the
Prussian army, and even gave to it a national character by assigning to every regiment a Prussian recruit-
ing district, from which two-thirds of its strength
were drawn: the conception was remarkable at a
time when every European army was a force of paid
(and often imported) pugilists. On the side of
civil administration Frederick William created the
centralized executive of the Prussian monarchy
and baptized it with the strikingly national title of
*General - Ober - Finanz - Kreigs - und - Domainen-
Directorium.* His remarkable blend of languages
and metaphors (*"Ich stabilire die Souveraineté wie
einen Rocher von Bronce"*) concealed a great truth;
in the army and the civil service Frederick William
had made the two wheels of the Prussian machine.
He Prussianized Prussia; and it seems almost time
that somebody called him a Hun.

The Prussianization of Germany was a far simpler,
if more gradual, process which filled the later half
of the Nineteenth Century. But its earlier years
are occupied by a curious business which almost,
but not quite, succeeded in producing the German-
ization of Prussia. Between 1815 and 1848 the militant agriculturists of Brandenburg were very nearly
reabsorbed in that German family whose natural
occupations are the carving of wood and the composi-

tion of music. Under Frederick William IV, who almost justified *Punch's* accusations of habitual intemperance by his persistent attachment to the mediæval ideal, the Prussian almost became a mild-eyed German rustic. But the Liberal revolution of 1848 put an intolerable strain upon the *Junker;* and the generous fever was succeeded by the cold fit of Manteuffel, until Bismarck restored to Prussia the normal circulation of its blood and iron. The historians of Prussia have amused their leisure by selecting certain figures as typical of that kingdom. One of the most popular for this purpose is Frederick the Great, who is constantly decorated with a distinction which he would have resented as an insult. But that cosmopolitan was the man of his century rather than of his country; he was equally typical of France, of Austria, of Spain, or even of England, because, in fact, he was only typical of the year 1760. There is a modern belief that the qualities of efficiency and organization are in some way Prussian; and the attempt has been made to sum up the North German character in the accomplishments of its commercial magnates. But the powers of industrial organization in time of war, which should have earned for the ingenious Herr Ballin the title of the North German Lloyd George, are hardly inherited from the Great Elector, and the praise of them should be attributed to a somewhat older race. The truth is that the business man is not a national type: Herr von Gwinner's attachment is not to the Old Mark, but to the new *mark*. Commercial aptitude is not an inherited, but an acquired characteristic; and its inclinations are as cosmopolitan as those of Mr. Henry Ford, whose attempted gift of what Lord Beaconsfield must have called "Peace with Rubber" intrigued the world from Kirkwall to Para. There is only one Prussian type, and he is called Bismarck.

The history of Prussia is the history of its successes; but there is perhaps more instruction to be derived from the record of its failures. It cannot colonize in hot climates: yet it seeks an empire overseas. It cannot govern subject races without alienating them as far asunder as the Poles: yet it seeks to revise its frontiers within Europe. It cannot manipulate a modern constitution: yet it claims that the advance of its frontier-stones is the march of civilization. It is a claim that must be denied.

SOME ROMANS

THERE is an admirable, if neglected, joke by the forgotten humorist who decorated the east front of the Colonial Office. This accomplished person, whose exquisite parodies of extinct statesmen in Imperial attitudes enliven the somewhat melancholy lives of the pelicans in St. James's Park, shared Nature's abhorrence of a vacuum. He flourished with tropical luxuriance about the year 1866, and disliked blank spaces. His treatment of them, which was generally either historical or vegetable, lapsed in one magnificent instance into the more facile method of allegory. Having punched a number of windows in the wall which separates the Colonial Secretary from the traffic in Whitehall, he proceeded to embellish the curved spaces about them, which a less fertile genius would have left empty, with several figures of young persons in the Victorian nude. These are well provided with those assorted fruits, cereals, steam locomotives, and spinning jennies which are known to mythologists as *attributes*. They are believed to represent continents, and the title of each continent is marked in plain figures underneath each immodest but symbolic person. There are six continents, and they are called Europe, Asia, Africa, America, Australasia, and Education: it is a profound allegory.

One should add that the last continent owes considerably less than its colleagues to the exploration of Englishmen. Indeed, it has never been satisfactorily ascertained whether the English mistrust Education because it is suspected of a connection with Lord Haldane, or Lord Haldane because he is feared to have had relations with Education. The sixth continent is, like Tunis, an odd place full of dates. Its sheds are all watersheds, and its gardens are all kindergartens. There are no songs there except the Gender Rhymes, and its literature has all been transposed (with the assistance of the late Dean Bradley) into *Oratio obliqua*. It is, in fine, a continent which is more at home in a University than in the narrower limits of the universe, and it belongs more obviously to the Montessori than to the solar system. That is the deluge of reflection that has been provoked by the erratic symbolism of a Victorian sculptor in a hurry to finish off his decorations in time for Mrs. Disraeli's At Home in the cold weather of 1867.

There is, on the face of it, no inherent reason why

one should not apply the geographical method to the examination of the works of man as well as to that of the wonders of Nature. The mind of Balzac is habitually described in terms of undergrowth and jungle by those indefatigable impostors who urge young men to read the whole *Comédie Humaine,* and are presumably forgiven because they know not what they do. The leading text-books on the Canon and Apocrypha of Mr. Conrad will inevitably divide his work into spring- and neap-tides; and although Mr. Wells will drive his editors off the earth into the trackless wilderness of astronomy, the commentators on Mr. Bennett's Pentapolis *papyri* will find geography to be a convenient frame in which to examine the camber of Trafalgar Road and the off-licence of the "Tiger." But of all the worlds in which the mind of an author has ever roamed, the most geographical is the world of Edward Gibbon. The setting of his piece is entirely the long curving background of the Roman frontier from Borkum to the Persian Gulf.

Almost the whole of Roman history is Roman geography. One may study the Republic (as indeed one can follow almost any Imperialist development) with a blank map and a pot of paint. Its record consists of a combined problem in mathematics and geography, showing how a city multiplied by an army became a peninsula, and how all three divided by a

navy turned into the Mediterranean seaboard. That
is where one finds Rome in the year 44 B.C., with the
provincial system roughly blocked out, and an attractive young woman of the name of Cleopatra wondering how she could get an introduction to a bull-necked
man with a low forehead, named Antony, whom she
had noticed making a rather noisy speech to a crowd
in the Forum over the body of her old friend Julius
Cæsar. At this point one leaves the Imperialist Republic, under which an aristocracy of army contract-
ors conducted an empire without a civil service, a line
of policy, or a system of defence; and one finds oneself, like Garrick between the Muses, led by Edward
Gibbon and Professor Bury down the primrose path
that leads to Romulus Augustulus.

Now, the history of the Roman Empire, unless
one is to regard it as a mere concatenation of rather
improper anecdotes, is the history of the Roman
frontier. For the first time in the history of the
Western world, policy turned inland. Ancient history, before the frontier-builders of the early Empire,
had been the history of littorals, and the history
of early commerce was the history of a coasting
trade and a few rivers. But with the Empire it
became a problem (it is a problem that was never
solved) to construct a military frontier that should
protect the Mediterranean basin upon the North-

east and the East. Augustus cleared the *glacis* of the Alps; and then, in the war in which Varus lost his legions, he attempted to open out to the line of the Elbe. The failure was acknowledged in the retreat, which was as complete as Napoleon's in 1814, to the line of the Rhine and in the organization of the provinces called, to the perpetual satisfaction of Mr. Belloc, the Germanies. In the wars of Germanicus the advance to the Elbe was again attempted; but Claudius called a halt. He was an author of plays, an admirer of Cicero, and a spelling-reformer; but he invented Secretaries of State and had an Imperial policy. The successive *pronunciamientos* which threw up Galba, Otho, Vitellius, and Vespasian interrupted the formation of the frontier, until the German *Limes* was formed across the angle between the lower Rhine and the middle Danube. Then an Andalusian named Trajan flung out the two great salients in the defence of which so much of the energy of the Empire was wasted: the salient of Bohemia in advance of the Danube frontier, and the salient of Irak, which was intended (if it was intended for anything) for the protection of Asia Minor by a singularly exaggerated outwork. After the effort of Trajan the armies of the Empire fell back; and the manhood of Western Europe entered on a defensive warfare of four centuries against the barbarians who

96

were to make the Middle Ages the admiration of clergymen, romantics, and architects.

That is the severe geographical skeleton upon which the history of the Empire should be constructed; and it is a piece of work which General Young —a gallant officer whose military views are full of interest and originality—would have been well qualified to produce. He is, however, as Mr. James would have said, so quite heroically "out" to rewrite Gibbon; and the General follows with all the advantages of senior rank in the familiar footsteps of the sceptical Major in the Hants Militia. He does not, however, go the whole Gibbon; his manner in anecdote lacks the metallic precision of his predecessor's, and he is somewhat oppressively on the side of the angels. There is an indignant protest in his Preface against the high value set upon the age of the Antonines. General Young is gallantly prepared to detect a heyday, which has hitherto escaped attention, between the terminal points of Constantine and Theodosius. If it is a healthy symptom (and every patriotic Englishman must hope that it is so) that one's art should all be shockingly out of drawing, there can be no doubt that he is quite correct. He is concerned to rescue Constantine and Gratian from the rubbish-heap and to denounce "the error which has styled the retreat of the Roman army from Persia in 363 a great disaster instead of a glorious feat of arms": it is curious how the climate prevailing in Irak perpetually renders obscure the precise result of military operations conducted in Mesopotamia. But in spite of his scholarship and the art of photography, the General reads (it is a compliment to both) more like Gibbon's ancestor than his descendant. The real truth is that there is no Gibbon but Gibbon, and Gibbon is his prophet. The solemn march of his cadences, the majestic impropriety of his innuendo are without rivals in the respective annals of British eloquence and British indelicacy; and the call for a new Gibbon is no stronger than that to which Mr. Mallock acceded when he put pen to paper to write a *New Republic.*

SOME LITERARY MEN

THERE is a government in the inner parts of Europe which has omitted to supply the customary statistical and dynastic information to the *Almanach de Gotha* and the *Statesman's Year Book*. It is called the Republic of Letters, and it forms the subject of frequent reference by Cabinet Ministers at public dinners given in honour of destitute literary men. It differs *toto cœlo* from that great Republic of the West, which we learned to know so intimately in the earlier stages of the war from the interception of its parcels post and the providential discovery of a German attaché's correspondence, called by patriots the Scrap of Papen; and it may be distinguished by the possession of three colonels (Colonel Maude, Colonel Roosevelt, and Colonel Newnham-Davis) from the Swiss Republic, which has, if one remembers the *affaire des colonels,* only two. It is notable to economists for a fiscal policy of more than Mercantilist fatuity, by which its balance of trade consists entirely of exports, and its constitution, which embodies lots of Legislature and no Executive, will bear comparison for pure anarchy with the late Republic of Poland, or with any settlement founded upon the principles of Brotherhood.

This neutral state, as innocent of belligerent intentions as Man before the Fall or Roumania before a decisive action on the Eastern front, was at one time the object of a sinister manœuvre of secret diplomacy: Mr. Shaw tried to bring it into the war. Its exquisite unsuitability for the purpose has been vividly summarized in a couplet of Mr. Shaw's own "Odalisque's Song" (one of the less familiar lyrics of his early manner):

"The Bosphorus is the boss for all
In this harem, harem, harem, harem, harem-scarum place."

But having resolved, apparently, to be remembered in history as the successful competitor of Dr. von Bethmann-Hollweg and Viscount Grey in the immolation of neutrals, he executed a *démarche* of consummate subtlety. Decorating the unsuspecting neutral state with the flattering name of *Intelligentzia,* which signifies, in the language of one of our late Allies, that arrogant minority which can both read and write, he invited it to assume control of England. A Ministry of All the Talents was to be substituted for a Coalition which it was charitable to suppose had once possessed some but had subsequently buried them; and Mr. Shaw would be enabled to gratify his long-cherished ambitions with the Lord-Lieutenancy and the resulting control of the Abbey Theatre. The ministerial appointments are at once obvious and attractive. Mr. Arnold Bennett as Chancellor of the Duchy of Staffordshire, Mr. G. K. Chesterton as Toastmaster-General, and Sir Thomas Beecham as Minister of Musicians slip naturally into their places. Mr. Hugh Walpole is a manifest First Commissioner of Wrexe; but more difficulty might be encountered in inducing Mr. Wells to accept the purely legal (and Hegelian) post of Lord Chancellor. And it is delightful to think of the House of Commons sitting for fifty-six hours in the half-darkness and watching the glow of Marlow's cigar, whilst Mr. Conrad answered a supplementary question about the disappearance of a Dutch consul in the Straits of Malacca; and to figure Mr. Belloc, who would be accommodated as Minister without portfolio because he had lost it somewhere, proceeding rapidly along the line R—R —R towards his room in the War Office is magnificent. But it is not the war.

It is an unfortunate fact that the Intellectuals are unfitted for executive posts. Their unsuitability for anything but a commentator's part is apparent from every one of their illuminating utterances. No great man ever knows what a war (or a peace) is about, because any person of intelligence tends inevitably to idealize its causes. He observes, when he is confronted with a war, an enormous and unparalleled dislocation of human existence; and he draws the intelligent conclusion that it is derived from a dispute of commensurate importance. That is precisely where in nine cases out of ten(and it was the object of our sincerest endeavours to persuade ourselves that our recent case was the tenth) the Intellectual is hopelessly wrong. He is wrong, because he is intelligent. If he were less intelligent, he would move from Golder's Green and be a statesman; and if he were less intelligent still, he would take a house in Kensington and be a Civil Servant. The causes of most wars have been grasped and stated by the officials who conduct them; and the man of light and leading must drop to the level of the leading article before he can understand them.

The attempt was made by several literary men to demonstrate that the last war was a war of ideas; but it was made without conspicuous success. That war, which was, in the words of George III, "bloody and expensive, but just and necessary," was a war of policies; and a policy with an idea in it is as inconceivable as an embassy with a *doctrinaire* in it. Neither in its origin nor in its conduct was the strug-

102

gle a war of ideas, unless it may be held to have acquired that character from the establishment of an Admiralty Board of Inventions in a shipping-office in Cockspur Street, where some distinguished admiral (with, it is to be hoped, the co-operation of Mr. Heath Robinson) sat waiting, like a sort of inverted Micawber, for something to turn down.

One has a perfect conviction that M. Paderewski never had a notion what Poland was at war for. He left that to an admirably named M. Grabski. It became equally manifest at an early stage that the most brilliant of our propagandists had failed to grasp the elements of England's case in the recent European argument. We were all to be congratulated on the return to controversy of that Gilbert whom (if it is not impertinent to say so) even Mr. Basil Hallam would have hesitated to call the Filbert. But only a hedonist would agree with a statement because he enjoyed it. Mr. Chesterton did not devote very much space to that enemy, in whom we all took such a growing interest since the time that his copper, oil and rubber increased in spite of the blockade. But having apparently formed what he himself calls the "unfortunate habit of publicly repenting for other people's sins," he filled a considerable space in apologizing for the misdeeds of England. His dramatization of history was founded on the simple and romantic scenario that a buffle-headed England is constantly enticed by a diabolical Prussia into opposition to a milk-white France. The characterization is so plain as to be almost caricature; and the drawing is so simple that it is merely *Simplicissimus*. One suspects that his loyalty to his French and Russian Allies was founded on the pleasing institution of the *pogrom* and the public degradation of Captain Dreyfus; and one detects in oneself a constant tendency to enjoy him without stopping to disagree. There is a brilliant parable of the Pan-German horse, which has been reading Houston Chamberlain and "discovers in the cat 'the characteristic equine quality of caudality, or a tail' "; and there is the startling suggestion that Italy declared war on Germany, which would have caused Baron Sonnino to faint in the arms of Signor Salandra.

But Mr. Chesterton will never secure a conviction on *The Crimes of England*. The first charge is that in or about the Seven Years' War the prisoner did unlawfully aid and abet one Frederick Hohenzollern *alias* the Great to break and enter the Holy Roman Empire and otherwise maltreat the Balance of Power. Mr. Chesterton's reading of British policy is that Chatham took England into the war merely to score off France; and he seems hardly to have noticed that the significance of the whole affair for England was not European at all, but Indian and American. The next count in the indictment is the long war against the Revolution and Empire. Here Mr. Chesterton has a noticeably better case, although he almost spoils it by an observation on the Low Countries, that eternal British *casus belli:*

It is very arguable that England must, in any case, have fought to keep her influence on the North Sea. It is quite equally arguable that if she had been as heartily on the side of the French Revolution as she was at last against it, she could have claimed the same concessions from the other side.

One is almost tempted to the angry impertinence that even if the Germans spell Culture with a K, that is no reason why Mr. Chesterton should spell Boche with an s.

SOME TURKS

THE Eastern or, as it is sometimes romantically termed, the old, old question originated in the days when the free and independent nationalities of Europe were snarling and scuffling in the ruins of the Roman Empire. Its solution, like the ballad style and the art of staining glass, is one of the things which the Middle Ages omitted to bequeath to the modern world, and by that omission tempted the Nineteenth Century to produce the Treaty of Berlin, the ballads of Mr. William Morris, and the north window of Rugby Chapel.

The Roman Republic, which had carried to a supreme height the arts of portrait-sculpture and street-fighting, left to its successor a territory including the entire Mediterranean basin; and the Empire, having added to its dominions during the reign of a lunatic some part of the British Isles, proceeded to protect its territory by the trace of the Roman frontier. The civilized world was converted into a single fortress

by a chain of fortified positions which followed the
lines of the Rhine, the Danube, and the Euphrates.
That fortress faced towards the East, because civilization was threatened solely by the surplus population
of Asia, and it became the business of the Roman
power to protect its outworks. The history of the
ancient world is the history of European resistance to
the Asiatic *Drang nach Westen;* and when this resistance failed to maintain against its enemies the line of
the Roman frontier, the history of the ancient world
came to a sudden and chaotic end. Europe passed
into "the filth and falsehood of the Middle Ages,"
as it was elegantly described by the Reverend Hugh
McNeile, in a speech on Church extension delivered
at Freemasons' Hall in the year 1839; and the power
of Islam, which had brushed away the Crusades like
a swarm of flies, entered Europe by the gate of the
Balkans. Constantinople went down like a rotten
tree; and whilst the first men of the Renaissance were
staring incredulously across the North Atlantic, the
Turks watered their horses in the Danube.

The Turkish question, which has been answered in
various tones from the elaborate irony of Lord Beaconsfield to the synthetic wisdom of the Conference of
London, is a successor in the direct line of a dozen
Eastern questions which were forced upon Europe by
the collapse of the Roman line. The Eastern March

of European civilization was protected by the successive efforts of the Franks, the Germans, the Czechs and the Poles; and it seemed sometimes that Christendom was almost united by the danger in the East, just as Gambetta sought to unite French republicans by the appeal *Regardez la trouée des Vosges.* It has been observed by sensitive historians that the destruction of European things comes always from the East; even M. Benedetti made his first public appearance as Secretary of Legation at Constantinople. Timur, Jenghiz, and Attila came upon Europe from the East; and this sinister succession has been responsible for a long series of sombre perorations. But it is perhaps pardonable to point out that barbarian invaders have come always from the East, because there was, prior to the discovery of America, nowhere else for them to come from.

It is almost five centuries since the Turkish question entered upon its European phase. When the fall of Constantinople substituted the organized effort of Islam for the random and seasonal raids of unco-ordinated barbarians, the problem was presented for solution in its acutest and most painful form. It did not vary in its factors between the collapse of the Genoese infantry in the year 1453 and the Victorian sensation of 1876, when Mr. Gladstone startled the readers of his pamphlets with the most

effective employment of foreign names in the English
language:

Their Zaptiehs and their Mudirs, their Bimbashis and
their Yuzbashis, their Kaimakams and their Pashas, one and
all, bag and baggage, shall, I hope, clear out from the
province they have desolated and profaned.

The writer's reference was to the province of Bulgaria, to which, if Amsterdam messages were to be
believed, the genial presence of the Bashi-bazouk returned during the late war in response to the cordial
invitation of the local authorities.

The problem set to European intelligence by the
Turkish Empire was in its elements a simple one.
The advance of the Ottoman Turks had encamped
upon European soil a deeply religious and highly
military people, who combined an enlightened mono-
theism with an ability to fight behind entrenchments.
In face of this power, which controlled Asia Minor,
the Balkan Peninsula, and the waters of the Black
Sea, two solutions were practicable; indeed, it is notable in political history as the sole conjunction of
events which did not inspire Mr. Gladstone to con-
front his countrymen with three alternatives. Either
the Turkish power might be stabilized by the French
(and later the German) policy of foreign commerce
and reform; or it must be driven out of Europe by

the Austrian (and later the Russian) policy of expulsion by armed force. The history of the Eastern question consists of the alternation of these two courses; and what our fathers used picturesquely to call the Concert of Europe was confined in its repertoire to variations upon these two themes.

The crusading efforts of Holy Russia form a familiar chapter of European history; but the Austrian phase of the Eastern question is a more neglected subject. The Austrian power was driven directly upon the alternative of expulsion by the great offensive of 1683, which had brought the Spahis of Kara Mustapha within sight of Vienna; and it became the object of the more intelligent advisers of the Emperor Charles VI to convert the Hapsburg monarchy into a Danubian power at the expense of Turkey. The memoirs of Prince Eugène, whose trilingual signature *Eugenio von Savoie* is a convenient indication of the cosmopolitan allegiance of Austrian statesmen, contains a remarkable picture of those Turkish wars in which the infidel displayed the courtesy of Saladin towards crusaders in periwigs. His Highness had a remarkable taste for sermons; and it may be doubted whether his aphorism *C'est le premier jour qu'on entre en campagne que le public doit être informé des alliances* would find any extensive favour with the Union of Democratic Control.

His taste for *de bien jolis airs d'opera-comique* was almost light-minded, and his opinion of the English ("I paid great court to Ministers. I gave presents, because England is a great country for buying.") is worthier of a disillusioned Whip than a distinguished stranger. But Eugène had a just appreciation of the Turkish genius for spade-work, which he believed them to have inherited from the Romans. If his theory is correct, it is by a delicious irony that the Osmanli have employed Plevna, Tchataldja, and Gallipoli to impress Europeans with the Roman tradition. The memoirs of Eugène are full of the characteristic names and actions of the Turkish wars:

> The Bashaw and the garrison were massacred. The Seraskier burnt Novigrad to the ground. . . . There was a Bashaw amongst our prisoners whom I questioned to no purpose upon the plans of Kara Mustapha; but the action of four Hussars, who stood with drawn swords ready to cut him to pieces, prevailed upon him to confess that Szegedin had been his object.

In a conversation held at Rastadt two years after Malplaquet Eugène gave to Villars a vivid picture of savage warfare on the lower Danube, where one met "their flanking Spahis with their cursed howls of *Allah! Allah!* and their trick of coming on by fifties round a little flag." This encounter of Viennese cosmopolitans with the militant theology of Asia was a

111

singular experience for the men of the Eighteenth Century; and it forms one of the queerest chapters in the history of the Eastern question.

That question may be studied from either of two angles. It is customary in Europe to follow the European side of the duel, and to trace the transitions by which the crusader's sword passed from Austria to Russia, and from Russia to the Balkan League. It is a line of study which enables one to appreciate Eugène's wise prophecy to his master in the year 1734 that the Serbs and Bosniaks would inevitably oppose the House of Hapsburg; and it affords the exquisite spectacle of Lord Beaconsfield congratulating his Peers on the well-founded opinion of Count Bismarck that "Turkey in Europe once more exists." But it is sometimes worth while to examine the problem of Turkey from the angle of Turkey. The experiment must seem almost as attractive as to examine the problem of evil from the angle of the Evil One; but it is worth making. Sir Mark Sykes, who will probably be known to posterity as the author of a perfect parody of the Drill-book, once made the attempt; and he is, in spite of a shocking conviction that history is really amusing, a most attractive historian. Some such foundation is urgently needed, if the Englishman who thinks about the Eastern question is to understand what the Turk thinks about the Western question. The Turk is usually the last person who is considered in those re-arrangements of his territory which are so generously undertaken by others on his behalf; and it is perhaps time to call him before the curtain, if only as author of the piece.

The historian's views on the problem of Armenia are a trifle startling in one of his nationality; he finds the Armenians profoundly unpleasing, especially when leavened by American missionary effort; he announces that "the Armenian national revival was a calamity which has not yet reached its catastrophe"; and he is inclined to agree with the unpopular opinion of the late Sultan Abdul Hamid that the removal of the Armenian question can only be effected by the removal of the Armenians. His real sympathy is for the Arab on the sufficient grounds that he is a mono-theist and a Fine Fellow; and one accepts with respect the opinions of a traveller whose journeys make the map of Asia Minor look like an illustration to the Acts of the Apostles.

But the foremost merit of Sir Mark Sykes as an observer is that, like James Morier, he appreciated the supreme absurdity of the East. It has been justly observed that there is nothing funnier than a foreigner; and the solemn imbecility of Orientals is one of the most delightful spectacles provided by

Providence for the entertainment of Englishmen. He met a Kurd, who expressed my own objection to being photographed, because "God only knows what is looking through those great eyes." His escort was commanded by a sergeant who had been sentenced, by the adorable fatuity of the East, to one hundred years' imprisonment for murder; and he met in the middle of a desert a genial little man who had got a hundred and fifty years for robbing the Alexandretta mail. As a Conservative, Sir Mark could appreciate the comedy of *Huriyeh,* the Turkish equivalent of *Liberté, Egalité, Fraternité,* which inspired young officers in 1909 to say *J'adore le jambon, je bois le koniak* in the frenzy of emancipation. But above all there is the pure farce of the Boundary Commission on the Turco-Persian frontier, which, finding itself totally unprovided with any form of map, was permanently and pardonably drunk. Asia is not a mystery, where sinister men with cruel eyes and queer crooked scimitars crouch and mutter round low fires in black Bedouin tents: Asia is one of the jokes that Europe cannot see.

SOME SERBS

IT was the Dictionary of Quotations (that great, if somewhat confused thinker) who said *Inter arma silent leges;* and it was never more obvious than in that saying that the Romans had not the advantage of our acquaintance. The moderns may have their weaknesses of principle and conduct; but it will stand always to their credit that they have given the lie to every proverb upon which they could lay hands. Ten minutes with the Defence of the Realm Regulations would have knocked the Roman aphorist off his proverbial perch. Since those summer holidays when five Powers went to war instead of going to the seaside, we have lived under what Professor Dicey would call the Rain of Law. The official imperative was never more categorical; the toga would appear to have forgotten its Ciceronian obligation to yield to the sword. On one afternoon in that first summer M. Noulens tabled in the French Chamber of Deputies eighteen *projets de loi:* it was the first *rafale* of the legislative "seventy-five." Great Britain, by the

combined energies of Parliament and the Privy
Council, produced in three months a Handbook of
Emergency Legislation which dwarfed a volume of
the Annual Statutes; and the Germans in Belgium
volleyed proclamations with a reckless profusion of
ammunition.

But no provisional enactment of the whole season
was more sensational than the decree by which the
Servian Government repealed Grimm's Law. It had
resulted from the sinister machinations of that phil-
ological Hun that the English for Servia was in
some danger of confusion with the Latin for slave;
King Peter's Minister at the Court of King George
was therefore authorized to announce to the panic-
stricken compositors of the English-speaking race
that "b" was no longer etymologically interchange-
able with "v." However ridiculous it may appear to
carry warfare into the alphabet, one was willing to
accede to every wish of a bitterly tried ally. But the
alteration represents, in one view, a considerable loss.
The name of Servia, which cannot connote servility
to any one except an ingenious schoolboy, stands in
history for the full record of a vigorous member of
the European family. If the past of Servia were dis-
honourable, one could have sympathized with the
change. But when one can hear in that name the
long roll of the wars against Turkey, one is unwill-

ing to let it pass out of the history of the war against the Magyar.

The historical mission of the Servian Empire in the days when Durazzo played Calais to Brindisi's Dover was to provide a buffer-state between Rome and Byzantium. It has been observed by railway engineers and Afghan statesmen that the principal qualities of a buffer are resilience and stability; and there seems no reason why Jugo-Slavia should not exhibit them when it is called on to perform the less heroic duties of buffer between Italy and Hungary. The problem of its reconstruction depends closely and entirely upon the past extent and present distribution of the race. We must be careful to reconstruct not any old Servia, but the historical Old Servia. Yet although you may permit a man to call Agram "Zagreb," it is not easy to surrender Spalato to the people who call it "Split." Since the Serb race occupies the north-western *massif* of the Balkan Peninsula, which has a littoral upon the Adriatic, it has been necessary at some points to modify the logical demands of strict ethnology in accordance with the political requirements of Italy, whose interest in that sea is supreme. But it was at least possible in an intelligent demarcation of Slav and Latin areas to eliminate the astonishing imposture of Albania. In so far as the Mpret's forsaken subjects were genuine Albanians, their autonomy represented a mildly satisfactory solution of a Balkan Ulster question. But when it was agreed between Rome and Budapest to endow that amazing creation with an ample coast-line and an Epirote province, it was a fraud upon Servia and Greece. In later life the deformed child of an unhappy marriage ceased to be even entertaining; and its death by the simultaneous amputation of Epirus and Valona left no mourners. England, by some fortunate miracle, possesses no Albania Society.

The history of modern Servia, like the history of modern Europe, begins in the age of the French Revolution. The Pashalik of Belgrade, after an interval of mild reform, was revisited in 1804 by the familiar circumstance of a Turkish massacre. An ex-officer of Austrian police, named George Petrovich, headed a national rising, which converted a provincial riot into a war of liberation and founded the royal house of Kara-George. When Napoleon marched the Army of England from the Boulonnais to the Danube, the Servian nation was little more than a religious conspiracy; in the year of Wagram it was a sovereign state. But four years later the reaction in Servia, as in Western Europe, returned in triumph. The national leadership had passed to Milosh Obrenovich, and in the rainy autumn of 1813, which saw Napoleon ride whistling into Leipzig, the

Turks returned to the disloyal Pashalik with the genial accompaniments of Spahi feudalism and famine. Milosh opened a second war of liberation in 1815, and Servia was more fortunate than France in its Hundred Days. Six months of war and fifteen years of negotiation secured Servian independence. The new State did not become, like Greece, the darling of Russian diplomacy; and the *enfants perdus* of English drawing-rooms, who were prepared to die for Ypsilanti in the name of Pericles, never fought the battles of Milosh Obrenovich. The Servian state came into existence by the leave of Turkey and without the humiliation of European assistance. The liberation of Italy, which had preached the principle *Italia fara da se,* was the work of Napoleon III; but the unaided *Risorgimento* of Servia was as creditable to its national effort as the military revelation of 1912, by which the Balkan monarchies demontrated to their disgusted patrons that they could walk alone.

The rise of Servia was an ungenial education in politics. It is the misfortune of "nations struggling to be free," when they lose the illusions of their youth, that they learn the advantages of opportunism. To that lesson the Serb added a natural aptitude for sudden death; and this combination, which brought him successfully through two European wars in eighteen

119

months, has helped him to survive a third. It is a drastic experience of almost uninterrupted warfare. One knows nothing of Serb humour except that it laughs "ha-ha" to the trumpeters.

The Anglo-Servian alliance was perhaps the queerest combination of the war which sent Sikhs to restore King Albert to Brussels and Australians to force the Straits for Russia. The Serb has made the bitter discovery that wars are won by man-power alone, and he has learnt in battle and pestilence the truth of the Biblical observation, "The sinews of war is death." That is why he was not an unworthy ally, and the alliance was not inconsistent with the tradition of British policy. Great Britain, by the policy of the Balance of Power, was the standing ally of small nations. It may be true that she prefers to keep them small, and that she takes little interest in her foreign relations when they cease to be poor relations. But it was by design and not by accident that she sided in the war with Servia and Belgium. The alliance of Belgium made a singular appeal to British opinion; it would be no more than justice if the name of Servia, which has won greater battles in the face of greater odds, were raised to an equal height.

SOME PEERS—I. LORD RUSSELL

THERE are few things more disappointing in English history than English revolutions. It is for the future to show whether John Tanner wrote the *Revolutionist's Handbook* in vain; but the revolutions of the past exhibit a dismal and domestic gift of never upsetting the national household. In the Great Rebellion the King left by the front door; in the Glorious Revolution he emerged from the tradesmen's entrance; and the Revolution of 1832 never happened at all. The Whig Party, having made the second and directed the third, spent the evening of its days in contemplation of itself, took to writing memoirs, and died in or about the year 1895. One may judge it as the President of the Probate, Divorce, and Admiralty Division judges his votaries—by reading their letters. The Russell letters are uniformly and magnificently Whig. They were manifestly written in the library corner near the bust of Locke. They are calm and spacious and full of Virgil, deliberate, and resigned with the resignation of men who governed England, because there were only about sixty-four real people in the country to do it.

But one must not belittle Russell, the gravity of the Twenties, and the honesty of the Whig Settlement. At the end of the Great War England found herself exposed to the full horrors of peace. The taxpayer discovered (the discovery is almost topical) that whilst he maintained such luxuries as an Army of Occupation in France and a policy of non-intervention, he could not see those sweeping reductions of taxation which had been his dream since Mr. Pitt, in February, 1792, anticipated "fifteen years of peace"; the farmer realized that War Office contracts were apt to terminate with wars; and the shipowner observed without enthusiasm the end of a blockade which had meant to him the monopoly of the world's carrying trade. The consequences were the stormy years from Waterloo to the Reform Bill, "an awful period," as Sydney Smith called it, the classical time of English Liberalism, his familiarity with which gives their chief value to Mr. Asquith's excursions into historical precedent. It had become traditional for the Whigs to conduct England's revolutions. But many of them approached the new problems in the temper of a family practitioner faced with un-authorized symptoms; and their management of the transition from bare oligarchy to a "sort of" democracy lacked the pantomime smoothness of the transformation scene of 1688.

It is now possible with the material that has been rescued from limbo to study the Whig in every stage of evolution, from the chrysalis of Lord Holland regretting "the vulgar and unjust abuse of Borough Mongers," because "the influence of property *must* exist, and I certainly think it is happy that it *must,*" to the developed democracy of the Reformers of 1832. The growth of Lord John Russell's views may be studied before a perfect background of Lord Holland and his own father: against such a background Lord John's colouring is anything but protective.

That singular little man was born six weeks before Valmy, and died in sight of the Treaty of Berlin; but his letters leave him in 1840, when a gentleman's collars were still as high as his principles, and Queen Victoria was young. It is a grave blow to the theory that expulsion from school is the necessary prelude to greatness to learn that Russell was "the best of all good little boys"; and as such he was invariably portrayed in *Punch*. Perhaps his editor has been unduly lenient in admitting the obsequious appreciations of his preceptors: the Georgian pedagogue is a little exhausting when he is on his best behaviour. The Peninsular letters are all interesting; not many young men have a European war for a feature of their holidays, and Russell's Spanish experiences were thoroughly instructive. At Edinburgh he was a persevering debater, and read papers on the Cortes with the air of an expert. More valuable was his inspection of Peninsular battlefields; and he never forgot in later political struggles the defensive qualities which he saw in Wellington at Torres Vedras. In the year of Leipzig he entered Parliament; and it is by a delightful irony that the Reformer first represented his fellow-citizens when he was a minor.

In 1814 he visited Elba and saw the Emperor, who had become temporarily a part of the Grand Tour. There is an account of their conversation. Napoleon informed the young man that there would be no war in Europe at present, explained the Saxon and Polish questions, and condemned the American War. In his Introduction the editor has secured interesting confirmation of the other recorded remark of Napoleon in the same conversation: the Emperor was of opinion that Wellington was aiming at the English throne, a brilliant illustration of his total inability to understand anything English. He had studied English history with infinite pains when he was in the Artillery; yet he had not learned that in England gratitude invariably takes the form of supersession. Napoleon's judgment in this instance was vitiated by a fatal familiarity with his own country, where great men were used, not shelved.

There are few revelations in these letters. But they are valuable for the sustained picture of the times, the Whigs, the countless Russells, and the growing realization that somewhere outside was the population of England.

II. LORD WELLESLEY

It was Mr. Kipling who discovered that proconsuls prance; and no one should know better. There is something about the temporary occupation of an Oriental throne that seems to unfit its tenants for a more even gait; and since high-stepping is unpopular in British politics, their later careers are often flavoured with a bitter taste of failure. When a satrap is returned empty from his province, there is no sadder sight than his continued efforts; Nature spares to extinct volcanoes the indignity of a prolonged activity on half-pay. There is no failure so dismal as a successful man; and the after-lives of viceroys have all the bitterness of fallen royalty without any of its faintly romantic quality. Of this depressing type the Marquess Wellesley is a conspicuous and familiar instance. He reached his greatest eminence in Calcutta before he was forty; and for the remainder of a long life he revolved gloomily round Dublin Castle and the Foreign Office in the hopeless endeavour to live within his reputa-

126

tion. A protracted bearing of the White Man's Burden not infrequently afflicts the carrier with a stiff neck and a high stomach. These are the industrial diseases of Empire; but they are fatal to the disabled worker's chances of subsequent employment: it is the Curzon touch. When a sub-tropical magnate returns to St. Stephen's on his way to Westminster Abbey, he is apt to discover that his gifts are more easily demonstrable from the Throne than across the floor of the House, and to observe with disgust the decline of the terror of the back-blocks into a supernumerary on the Front Bench. In that position a man falls back upon his education. He will begin by reading Thucydides for political purposes. But a very few years will see him translating Catullus. When he cannot speak, he reads; and when he can no longer read, he writes. It will always be significant that Wellesley published his *juvenilia* at the age of eighty.

The accident of birth has cast across all his achievement the long shadow of the Duke of Wellington: one should not have eminent brothers, if one proposes to be eminent oneself. Wellesley lived his life under a fraternal cloud which he shares with Quintus Cicero and Mr. Gerald Balfour. But it is possible to discern beneath it a tolerably brilliant career. He emerged after a polite education into the world of Irish politics, and entered the Irish House of Lords in the days when Dublin was a capital, before Mr. Pitt had established the money-changers in its Parliament. His observations on the subject of Irish volunteers are not uninteresting, since volunteering is once more the vogue west of Holyhead. "The assembly of the volunteers," he informed the House in 1783, "has sat for nearly three weeks with all the forms of Parliament; and will any noble Lord say that they have no intention to infringe the privileges of Parliament and to attempt the total extinction of the laws of the land?" And fifteen years later he received from Lord Auckland a report that is even more topical: "The Orange Boys, as they are called in Ireland, are growing numerous (above 30,000) and are most inveterate against the United Irish. They are a dangerous species of ally; however, to a certain degree it is necessary to use them." Truly Ireland is as unchanging as the East.

Twelve months after his Irish début Mornington secured the support of a minimum of Devonshire freeholders, and appeared in the House of Commons as a member for Beer. Like all young men with a future, he specialized in a remote subject, and delivered a maiden speech on the Indian adminis-tration of Warren Hastings. Nine years later he obtained recognition as a Privy Councillor and

Commissioner of the Board of Control. In those days the road to the East lay through Leadenhall Street, and young men who commended themselves to the Company might look forward with confidence to a wealthy middle age. He was now involved in an elaborate manœuvre for high office; a great part of his correspondence consists of letters whose sole value is that they display the working of the machine of patronage. But there comes a point at which a diet of loaves and fishes is cloying to the historian; the eternal feeding of the multitude, which was the main business of the Eighteenth Century, is a monotonous spectacle, and the editor can do little to provide us with a change of scene. Eventually, after a protracted campaign across the Front Bench and up the back stairs, Mornington obtained his deserts, and became Governor-General of India with an English peerage and the title of Baron Wellesley. The Meredithian interlude of his private life was closed by his marriage with Mademoiselle Roland; and he sailed for India by the Cape, leaving his wife to look after his children and his country to deal as best it could with the French Revolution. From 1797 to 1805 he played with distinction the part for which he had been cast by Mr. Pitt, whilst his brother earned under him an increasing reputation as a Sepoy General. His correspondence at this period is less interesting than at almost any other; he was kept posted by friends at home in the course of European affairs, and he sent in return dissatisfied portraits of Anglo-Indian society, "so vulgar, ignorant, rude, familiar, and stupid as to be disgusting and intolerable; especially the ladies, not one of whom, by-the-bye, is even decently good-looking." Perhaps it would be unkind to add that the East is as unchanging as Ireland.

These sorrows of monarchy do not weigh hardly on kings, because kings are necessarily semi-educated; but Wellesley was an able man and felt his position acutely. In 1800 Wellesley received the crowning insult of a step in the Irish peerage—his "double-gilt potato"—and his temper, which was being tried in the attempt to reconcile Leadenhall Street to the forward policy of the Mahratta War, descended from high wrath to puerility. Six years later he landed in England as a sort of *Scipio Asiaticus,* and re-entered the eternal game of Cabinet-making. In 1809 he made an effective appearance in Spain as Ambassador to the Junta and applied his imperative diplomacy to his languid ally; and on his return, since foreign policy was Spanish policy, he was very properly promoted to the Foreign Office. In his correspondence as Foreign Secretary there are two passages of supreme interest: a long review of the European and American situation which he submitted to Wellington in 1811, and the romantic story of an attempt to rescue Ferdinand VII of Spain from his French prison, in which British war-ships flit up and down the Breton coast and Ven-déan veterans roam in a mysterious darkness. In 1812 he resigned because of undue economies effected in the provision for the Peninsular War, and survived by thirty years the date at which his career ceased to possess any but a private interest.

III. LORD NORTH

THE statesman who conferred upon the habitable globe the inestimable benefit of the United States has awaited his biographer for one hundred and twenty years. He has seen Chatham become a legend and Charles Fox a complete literature, whilst his own record was confined to the perfunctory invective of text-books and the comic relief of lecture-rooms. Probably he has regarded the circumstance with complete equanimity. If his life had been written twenty years ago, he would have received a severe whitewashing; and that is a degradation which he has eventually been spared. Nothing is more humiliating to a Borgia than to figure in a collection of *Quiet Lives of the Renaissance;* and a rehabilitation of North's gloriously shot-scarred reputation would have been like a wanton restoration of Fountains Abbey.

North and his kind, moreover, form a splendid part of the English tradition. The combination of high office with frank incapacity is peculiar to these islands; and it is unpatriotic to pretend otherwise. It is only foreigners, decadent Latins or unwieldy

Teutons, who have to seek out able men to be their governors. It is the first glory of the English system that it can support in office anything with two arms and a head, even though its governor gesticulates and gyrates as wildly as the governor of a steam-engine. Lord North was of the Bull-dog Breed; he made considerable contributions to the Rough Island Story. He was an Absent-Minded Beggar.

His clear-sighted biographer has no nonsense about his noble subject. He does not suggest that the loss of the American Colonies formed part of a far-seeing scheme for increasing the Empire by African expansion and the endowment of North scholarships in American universities. He does not pretend that North was handsome or eloquent or profound. One is left with the picture of a humorous fat man, who slept on the Treasury Bench and made jokes about himself. North had the Ministerial manner and a gift for repartee. As the Minister of George III, when the King had frankly established an absolutist system of personal Government, he had the courage of his master's convictions. His courage, which lasted until at the news of Yorktown he flung up his arms like a shot man, makes him a less ignoble figure than Newcastle, the other incapable Minister of the century. He weathered as severe a storm as the younger Pitt; and nobody has ever written songs about him.

He entered Parliament in 1754 as member for Banbury; and in his later career he became preeminently a House of Commons man. His neat little jokes, his habit of unabashed somnolence, and the easy insolence of his Ministerial manner endeared him to that singular assembly. The House preserves many reputations from the rougher handling of the country, and it appears to prefer its heroes slightly ridiculous. North fulfilled its requirements completely. In five years he was a Lord of the Treasury, and in the race for high office he was only ten years behind the younger Pitt. North became Chancellor of the Exchequer at thirty-five: but no one ever says so. It is true that he was only appointed because Charles Townshend was dead; but, after all, Mr. Goschen was only appointed because Lord Randolph Churchill was forgetful.

North's reputation was blasted by the American War of Independence. He did not find a solution for the problem of colonial taxation, and he failed to reconquer with a small professional army a continent on the other side of the world. This indictment is not unanswerable. In his policy he was in complete agreement with the majority of his countrymen, and in his conduct of the war his defeat was inevitable and not criminal. He even deserves his country's gratitude. By the American War he relieved England of an intolerable incubus of disloyal colonies. If a heaven-sent Whig had intervened in 1775 and averted the rupture, the colonists would undeniably have broken away twenty years later, when England was confronted with the simultaneous and graver menace of the French Revolution. To that double shock the country must have succumbed, and it was North's statesmanship which by a brilliant, if unintentional, stroke saved the State. He is one of the Empire Builders, even though he built largely by knocking down and wholly in his sleep.

IV. LORDS LYONS AND CLARENDON

THE worst consequence of the pernicious habit of reading is the loss of one's illusions. The truth about diplomacy is the most disappointing thing in Europe. One has been brought up by generations of dramatists to believe it to be an Olympian intercourse of elderly (but still attractive) gentlemen, their shirt-fronts barred with a ribbon of a primary colour and their conversation starred with a coruscation of unappropriated epigram. Diplomacy was the only possible occupation for Ouida's heroes when they were past work. It was a splendid and exclusive world, where all documents were secret and every *mot* was the *mot juste,* a sort of international Belgravia, where repartees settled the fate of nations. As a profession it became, after the disappearance of the smuggler, the last refuge of romance. A career of patriotic leisure and the combination of a title with the habit of constant untruthfulness served to surround the diplomatist with a romantic halo, whose radiance was undimmed by the fact that it was stereotyped. Now we know better; we are wiser and proportionately

136

sadder. Autumn winds of reality have blown upon our diplomats, and the *feuilletons* are falling. They are found to be a persevering class of the most voluminous leader-writers in Europe. Sometimes they call their leading articles Despatches and send them home. Sometimes they call them Notes and read them to one another: then there is a war. They dislike decorations, eschew mysterious exits, and disapprove strongly of mendacity. They even work. They manage these things better in Sardou.

Apart from this dismal revelation, one may learn a good deal from the study of these two gentlemen, one a great ambassador and the other a considerable Foreign Secretary. Both are strongly impressed with the characteristics of British diplomacy. It has no tradition and an abundance of good stories. It has not, with the exception of the control of the Low Countries and the road to India, any constant objective; and it is not unified in its history by the presence of any such authorized canon of policy as made Russian ministers for two centuries the executors of the will of Peter the Great. But it makes up admirably into volumes of memoirs.

Lord Lyons, who is remembered almost entirely for his twenty years' embassy in Paris, began life at the age of ten as an honorary midshipman. He abandoned these arduous duties in favour of a classical education; but he retained throughout life an appearance of the admiral that he so nearly became. His first mission of importance was to Washington, where he represented Great Britain through the Civil War. A considerable interest attaches to his correspondence during that bewildered struggle between two hostile forces, distinguishable only by the fact that one side wore the hats of dustmen, the other side the hats of postmen. It is a period with which the efforts of military writers and the cinematograph are making us increasingly familiar; and Lyons' interpretation of the American temper reveals an acuteness that was belied by his John-Bullish exterior. There is a delightful comment of Lord Palmerston on "the defeat at Bull's Run, or rather at Yankee's Run," which observes that "the truth is, the North are fighting for an Idea chiefly entertained by professional politicians, while the South are fighting for what they consider rightly or wrongly vital interests." In 1865 Lyons went for two years to Constantinople, and although he was not one of the great Near Eastern diplomats, at least he was more intelligent than Lord Stanley. The assertion of Lord Stratford de Redcliffe, that veteran viceroy of the Near East, that "Austria would be a safer neighbour to the Porte, even the whole length of the Danube, than either Russia or an independent Union," makes queer reading in these days, when the *Drang nach Salonik* is ancient history and indigenous populations scramble for Silistria. It is interesting to learn that King Edward in 1866 was strongly anti-Turkish; he was an unlikely Gladstonian at any time, and his position at home must have been curious, when Queen Victoria and Lord Beaconsfield were sitting cross-legged and sending Sikhs to Malta for the support of Abdul Hamid.

From Constantinople Lyons went to Paris, where he remained until his death twenty years later. He obtained the first embassy in Europe at the age of fifty, and his career became a reflection of French history from the Prussian War to the Schnaebele incident. He was an intelligent observer of the Prussian menace, although he could not spell Bismarck's name, and of the prelude to the war. Clarendon's unsuccessful effort to secure disarmament was made through him; and his reports to London in the hot weather of 1870 startled his superiors. Lord Granville wrote: "Your telegram of yesterday arrived while we were debating the Land Bill. It took Mr. Gladstone and me by surprise." It was the day that Benedetti arrived at Ems. On the same day Mr. Goschen presented a Report of the Select Committee on Local Taxation. It was printed a week later, on the day of the declaration of war: it is a glorious reflection. His intimate contact with French politics, from Gambetta and Grévy to Ferry and Boulanger, makes his later career a satisfactory and much-needed British supplement to M. Hanotaux's obstinately unfinished work. It is queer that Jules Ferry should have hungered for a *coup foudroyant* against China; it was the phrase which had sent the army of Châlons to Sedan. His recitation of Byron, his sense of humour, and his taste for jam (which only retreated before his final determination to join the Roman Church) mark him as a model uncle. He had the habit of identifying footmen by their calves, and once fought Leighton with pillows. And he was a great ambassador.

Clarendon had this in common with Lyons, that he spelt Bismarck without his "c." But what in Lyons was an error, was in Clarendon the proper protest of a Whig, against the ridiculous orthography of foreigners' names. His biographer admirably conveys the Whig view of the Continent, when he juxtaposes the following entries in his analysis of a chapter:

Marriage of Lady Constance Villiers to the Hon. F. Stanley . . . . 31*st May*, 1864.

Austria and Prussia occupy Holstein and Schleswig . . . . *February*, 1864.

That is the way we taught those foreigners to keep their places. Clarendon moved in the highest Whig circles; some of his correspondents are even a trifle supercilious about the House of Hanover, as when

Miss Emily Eden saw "the firm of Wales, Cambridge, and Greece" shooting in Richmond Park, and observed that "when the Duke of Cambridge lets himself out in a loose shooting coat, I think he reminds me of the dear lost Henry VIII."

Clarendon's career began with a picturesque Ministry at Madrid; but his importance rests on ten years passed at the Foreign Office. In the course of his two terms he declared war against Russia, signed the Treaty of Paris, and failed to prevent the Franco-Prussian War; it is a full record. His seven years' embassy at Madrid in the Thirties took him into the most confused and penniless period of Spanish policy. Ferdinand, who had closed the University and endowed a school of bull-fighting, was dead; the Regent governed for Isabella; and Christinos fought promiscuously against the Whites. A Mr. George Borrow was selling Bibles and getting himself into trouble with the authorities; Clarendon intervened, although he was discouraged by the "impossibility of defending with success all Mr. Borrow's proceedings," and succeeded in extracting Mr. Borrow from gaol. Politics were in the hands of a democracy of emotional sergeants, and political promotions were providing the Spanish army with an enormous corps of generals and a disappearing supply of subalterns. And through it all the people of Spain continued to smoke cigarettes;

141

the officers of the Spanish Navy availed themselves of the royal permission to act as licensed fishmongers in the harbour in which their commands were laid up; and Clarendon contemplated matrimony.

His second term at the Foreign Office possesses a more European interest. He is still a Whig, supercilious about Mr. W. E. Forster's "rough Yankee sort of exterior"; but he has larger topics to consider. The Prussians are in the Duchies, and Lord John Russell is graciously of opinion that "Bismarck is very amusing with his baby fleet." Twelve months later the Duke of Cambridge writes about "the horrible needle-gun," and Clarendon believes that "everything plays into L[ouis] N[apoleon]'s hands." The man who could so misread Sadowa was not likely to avert the war of 1870. He attempted to disarm Europe six months before Sedan. Bismarck said, in a compliment to his daughter, that he would have succeeded if he had lived; it was a graceful remark, but it is questionable history. Sir Herbert Maxwell has adorned the valuable pages of his biography with a quantity of elegant extracts from the classics; those which are in a dead language he charitably translates. It is perhaps as well that the war of 1870 lay outside his scope: it is the one thing in history which approaches Æschylus, and nothing would have satisfied Sir Herbert short of the bodily quotation of the entire *Persæ*.

SOME LAWYERS

AN ancient and, judged by contemporary standards, an honourable profession has long made its home in the Temple, once described (doubtless in anticipation of the event) as a den of thieves. The traffic of the metropolis goes round and (in the case of the District Railway) underneath this haunt of ancient strife; and its precincts—the Temple has always been credited with the possession of precincts—are undisturbed by the thunder of urban life. It is in the world of London, but not of it, an aloofness that stands in singular contrast to the thrusting persistence with which its professional population has steadily permeated, with none too peaceful penetration, the lives of their fellow-countrymen. Other trade unions have dictated the price of our bread, the warmth of our firesides, and the specific gravity of our beer. But it was reserved for the oldest, the narrowest, and the most powerful of the guilds to tamper with the quality of our jokes. There is about the vast majority of legal facetiæ a quiet but sustained ghastliness that has earned the candid detestation of the lay public; and it is a tribute to the slow charm exhibited by the *raconteur* of a recent collection to say that it will really bring illumination to all who wish to find out what exactly these lawyer fellows are up to, and that it will be read by them, not only with useful instruction on the ideals of a great profession, but with rare enjoyment of good stories. And, if one of these lawyer fellows may say so, the compiler has deserved well of the little republic of the law by interpreting its ideals, its standards, and its manners and customs in a way that should leave no excuses for future misunderstanding.

He quotes with indignation Disraeli's summary of the legal career as "port and bad jokes till fifty, and then a peerage." But he expresses his gratitude for having escaped the infliction of a peerage by sparing his public the corresponding infliction of bad jokes. The flow of anecdote under which he conceals the serious business of describing the legal world is a delightful stream in which one may fish in a random way for pearls. Any trustee will thrill with sympathy at the story of the examiner who said:

My rule is to pass a man who gets fifty per cent. of full marks. Now, I asked him two questions. The first was, "What is the rule in Shelley's case?" He answered that it had something to do with poetry. Well, that was wrong.

The second was, "What is a contingent remainder?" He answered that he was sure he didn't know. Well, that was right, and so I passed him.

That, of course, is precisely what a contingent remainder is.

And no litigant whose counsel has, after the manner of counsel, persistently misnamed him throughout the conduct of a case, will be able to withhold the tribute of a cheer (which will, in the ancient ritual, be instantly suppressed) at the bitter cry of the Judge:

Mr. Attorney, so long as you consistently called the plaintiff, whose name is Jones, by the name of Smith, and the defendant, whose name is Smith, by the name of Jones, the jury and I could follow you; but now that you have introduced the name of Robinson without indicating in any way whether you mean it to refer to the plaintiff or to the defendant, or to both indifferently, we are beginning to get bothered a bit.

The truth is, however disrespectful one may feel about the unsuitability of trade union jokes for the general public, that the jokes of the great trade union of the law are universally applicable. There may be—there indubitably are—tales of a technical and slightly carboniferous character about hairbreadth "escapes" that get roars of laughter at the annual meeting of the Gasfitters' Finishers' Union. The Textile Workers may wipe their eyes and waggle their hands feebly over a perfectly excruciating story about jacquards and hackling pins; and the Union of Journalists may (for all that I know) have their little jokes. But so few of us are gasfitters, or weavers, or (really) journalists, that the points of their professional humour whizz harmlessly overhead, like the spears in Homer. But we are all, in so far as we are debtors, creditors, tradesmen, customers, husbands, fathers, sons, or ratepayers, members of the great society of the law, even omitting the smaller, esoteric group of the barristers, solicitors, and jurymen. The law is at once the fairy-godmother and the wicked uncle of contemporary English life. Without it there would be no marrying or giving in marriage, no burglaries, street accidents or assaults, no bankruptcies or arson, no bigamy or perjury, nor any of those interminable police mysteries or "breezes in Court" which are the salt of modern life. Great is the law, and—against whatever competing topics—it will prevail.

SOME RICH MEN

ALMOST half of our current literature (including *vers libre* and the Law Reports) deals with the alluring topic of wealth. The fiction of the subject is, of course, mainly written by Mr. Arnold Bennett. But even in the bleak region of fact there is a whole group of periodicals which, nominally devoted to making public the *arcana* of the cinema industry, set themselves hebdomadally to disclose to awe-struck housemaids the immense sums of money earned by those more favoured members of their sex whose life is spent in grimacing at "close-ups" or in escapes from drowning (with real water). It is the income of these agile young ladies, rather than their pet iguana or their gymnastic accomplishments, which engages public attention; and a mass of odd publications ministers to this strange interest. Even the austere art of letters has been infected by this curious enquiry; and there are now several papers in which one may periodically gratify one's curiosity as to the income of one's favourite writer. An earlier

147

generation was satisfied with the simpler information that he had recently completed his Loamshire home at Little Sneethings, that he was never without a pocket Horace, that he was happiest on the home-farm among his pigs, and that in his tweeds he looked every inch a novelist. These tepid *personalia* were enough for our fathers. But their sons, anxious (as they are always proclaiming themselves) to get down to brass tacks, want something more. The age of Leverhulme and Zaharoff is not prepared to admire a writer for his style, or for his wife's connections, or even for his chintz and fumed-oak drawing-room. They want to know how much the fellow makes out of it; and their eager questionings are answered by the modern literary Press, which week by week unfolds the new plutocracy of letters. It is supremely successful, because it has found the exact measure of our interests. We all want, however much we may conceal our craving, to know about rich men—even if they write books.

The bibliography of this pleasing subject has come latterly to consist of a series of almost uniform biographies of wealthy people. They follow, in most cases, a pattern which is rapidly becoming monotonous. Readers of these works are rarely troubled with that opening chapter, which deals, in terms familiar to all students of biography, with

the absorbing topic of Ancestors; because the subjects of this class of appreciation rarely have any.
The more usual opening is a section upon Early
Struggles, in which the infant Crœsus begins to
exercise his famous aptitude for making money upon
the unpromising material afforded by his humble
beginnings. Follows a strenuous interlude in the
commercial arena (with personal appreciations by
his private book-keeper, the trustees in his first and
second bankruptcies, and the local Commissioners
of Income Tax), and the slow dawning of the
glorious day which saw his baronetcy, the Royal Visit,
and the final splendours of the Gilded Chamber.

But some of them are not quite like that. One
exception was George Cadbury. In the first place,
he insisted obstinately upon having ancestors, quite
interesting ancestors. One of them was killed at
Bannockburn, a scandalous departure from the
family's otherwise blameless record in relation to
small nations. Another learned the German flute;
but he subsequently deferred to family protests and
discarded this sensual instrument. George Cadbury's
father set the tone of social service, which has
happily become hereditary, with a vigorous campaign against the abomination of "the climbing boys"
who swept the chimneys of the Industrial Revolution.
And so the course was open for the clear-eyed

149

young visionary who entered the world in 1839 and remained in it until last year. His first step was to postpone his vision for a few years and to build up, with his brother Richard, a business which, measured by worldly standards, was highly successful. Their effort was made in the golden age of commercial endeavour, when the twin figures of Samuel Smiles and John Stuart Mill beamed down on private enterprise from the starry empyrean of Victorian economics. Their product rose by stages from "a comforting gruel . . . only one-fifth of it was cocoa, the rest being potato starch, sago flour, and treacle," until it reached those heights of perfection to which only the imagination of trained advertisement-writers can follow it. The business turned several awkward corners; the world became slowly aware of the name of Cadbury; and the happy members of the firm were able to devote themselves to the dispersal (which interested them far more than the accumulation) of their fortunes. That is, perhaps, the feature which distinguishes this career from other studies of successful men. Its chronicler was able to write a chapter on "The Spending of Wealth," a topic on which few biographers of millionaires could embark without a blush.

The whole interest of the story lay in the picture of nineteenth-century good works, upon which George

Cadbury entered with enormous gusto. Adult schools, meeting-houses, and model villages poured from his cornucopia on a startled community, as he returned once more to his vision and followed (as Lord Tennyson wrote of a far less deserving magician) the gleam. It is a queer and rather impressive spectacle, in which one may see a lively epitome of Victorian social endeavour. The magnificent impulses of his generosity were all kept well within the frame of the existing social order. His boldest experiments in industrial organization rarely strayed into a region beyond the charts of strictly private enterprise. But within the limits of his age he worked with astonishing vigour for social justice; although it is with a faint shock of surprise that one learns from his biographer that "he dreamed of the Merrie England where the old passion for wholesome revelry was recaptured." One is left with a sneaking fear that, in the long run, the wholesomeness might have exceeded the revelry.

His political career was full of interest. Birmingham in the middle of the last century was an unrivalled field for public spirit; and when his interests expanded into national politics, one gets a sudden view of those distant peaks, beneath which lie the hidden sources of the Nonconformist Conscience. His interest was in principles rather than in causes; and although a thorough Liberal, his principles impelled him both to refuse the offer of a seat by Mr. Gladstone and to assist the Independent Labour Party in its early days because "we want a hundred working men in Parliament." His own attitude was fundamentally that of the Free Churches, and even in the strange days of December, 1916, he was writing to his son:

As thou knows, I have always had some fear lest Lloyd George should be led away by his popularity, but so far he has remained loyal on essential principles; he is still not ashamed to be a Free Churchman; he still has the courage to attack England's greatest foe, the liquor traffic. . . .

That is a significant voice, because it puts into words one of those illogical, half-formed notions which determine the course of English politics. And yet one wonders (*pace* Lord Rosebery, who once called the Lord Protector "a practical mystic," and Mr. Gardiner, who said the same of Mr. Cadbury) whether it is precisely what Cromwell would have said.

One has throughout the picture of an earnest, cheerful man making a great business, reading prayers, directing newspapers, or writing little notes to his children about the servants and the garden. On the Continent they would see in him only one more example of the invincible hypocrisy of the

English.   No foreigner, one proudly feels, would possibly comprehend the strange blend of spiritual and temporal which makes up Nonconformity. But then foreigners are so logical.

SOME REVOLUTIONARIES

IN days when every newspaper reader is necessarily something of a connoisseur in revolutions, and Macaulay's schoolboy (if he is still alive) could tell us the precise distinction between a bread-riot, an *émeute,* and a *pronunciamiento,* it is refreshing to be taken back to the original source of all revolutionary inspiration, and to walk once more through the hot French summers of the years between 1789 and 1794. One was growing a trifle weary of the mechanical vulgarity of modern revolutions, with their motor lorries and machine guns and confusion in the telephone exchanges; and the return to the pikes and simplicity of the French primitives is a delightful experience. One may even hope that a revival of interest in the *Primavera* of revolution may give us a Pre-Leninite Brotherhood.

But, to say truth, the excursion, as one makes it with the modern historian for guide, is a trifle explanatory; and as this indomitable expositor hurries the eager amateur of the Revolution round some fa-

miliar corner, he is almost apt to recapture that ungrateful desire to be left alone in the Chamber of
Horrors which must so often have swept over Dante
as he toured another Inferno with another (and still
more distinguished) cicerone. It is enough for most
of us, when the overture falls silent and the curtain
rises on that broad and lighted stage on which the
Revolution was played out, to sit quiet in our stalls
and to watch the unrolling of the great—the greatest
—drama. But such sedentary inactivity as this hardly
suffices for the heroic temper of a Mrs. Webster. Avid
of explanations, she must be up and doing among the
scene-shifters; she threads her way through the stage-
crowds, interrogates the property man, and drags her
gaping readers through the *coulisses* of the Revolution, as she tracks down one after another of the
secret factors that lie behind the familiar frontage of
its history.

The plain truth about the Revolution is that it just
happened; and the study of that happening should
be enough for most of us. One may study it without
either the *manie de l'inédit* which impels the indomitable M. Lenôtre to give us foot-note biographies of all
the people who were passing along the street outside
a building where something was really happening, or
the engaging persecution mania with which the latest
of its historians tears off the mask of history.

In sympathetic obedience to a strong contemporary tendency, she finds German influences at work in the causes of the explosion. Marie Antoinette, the inevitable heroine of the piece, appears as a sound anti-German, who is consequently victimized by Prussian diplomacy; and the *Illuminati* devote an early Fabian subtlety to the task of plunging France into pre-Bakuninist anarchy. But the greatest efforts of her ingenuity are reserved for the unmasking of the Orleanist plot. Philippe Egalité, who normally appears on the revolutionary stage as a mild buffoon, is cast for a sinister, but leading, part; and the whole tide of the Revolution, in this new philosophy, is drawn after him by that moon-faced man. Writing with the full gusto of a Bonapartist pamphleteer under Louis Philippe, our lady detective finds the Orleanist hand active on every side. The party, which was apparently organized under the disreputable lieutenancy of Choderlos de Laclos, is made to include the most mixed revolutionary company: Mirabeau, Danton, Marat, Camille Desmoulins, Dumouriez, and Manuel all appear in Orleanist livery; and the food shortage of '89, the riots which preceded the storm of the Bastille, and the *journée* of June 20, 1792, are all attributed to this novel power of evil. Such an analysis of the secret causes of revolutionary events is profoundly interesting to connoisseurs of the Revolution. But it

156

hardly produces a narrative of events that is suitable for the novice who cannot distinguish the *Veto* from the *Maximum*. And one sometimes wonders, as one reads her ingenious exposition of how one statesman worked the rain-barrel while a colleague was busy producing rolls of thunder from the tin trays, whether the storm which blew down half the barriers in Europe was really a mere triumph of theatrical effects.

This Mrs. Webster is a trifle unfortunately inclined to treat the merits of the Revolution as a subject that is still open to discussion. Her authorities are sometimes stigmatized as "pro-revolutionary writers"; and one is tempted to ask whether the historians of the Flood should be similarly classified as "pro-diluvian" and "anti-diluvian." She sometimes handles her great men with a regrettable tone of aunt-like irritation, which betrays her into describing Robespierre as a "quarrelsome nonentity," and missing the great point of Mirabeau behind what she airily terms his "gigantic humbug." And she is tempted in an epilogue to adorn her tale with some extremely dubious morals. From the mildly astonishing conclusion that "the immense reforms brought about during the revolutionary era were not the result of the Revolution; it was to the King and his enlightened advisers . . . that the reforms in government were primarily due," she proceeds to the more perilous consideration of the present discontents. "Pacifists and Internationalists" catch it, as **Mr. Henry James** would have said, so quite beautifully hot; and the economic breakdown of Eastern Europe is heroically attributed to the machinations of "cosmopolitan Jewish financiers, who hope by the overthrow of the existing order to place all capital beneath their own control." This state of mind is on a par with the anti-German fervour of her "O for the touch of a Hidden Hand" on almost every page of history. One is reminded of the narrow temper of that war-time patriot who wished to abolish German measles and to rename it *Pox Britannica.* This passion for the detection of plots at all costs, which is an official merit in policemen and an entertaining accomplishment in the by-paths of historical research, may become, if it is left unchecked, an obsession leading to that political persecution mania, which is the obsession of so many bright contemporary minds.

AN AMERICAN

YOUNG James Gallatin was an American who talked about waffles and terrapin; but, unlike many Americans, he had ancestors. On the father's side James was a Swiss aristocrat, which his people felt acutely. In a passage of more than Trans-atlantic snobbery his father warned James, if he decided to remain in America, "never above all things to forget his birth and the duties that birth brings, always to be civil, particularly to those who were not his equals": there were to be no flies on James. But in the dazzle of his ancestors one had almost forgotten his father. Now Pop was an American diplomat, and thereby hangs an essay by Lord Bryce. Albert Gallatin was one of the solemn gentlemen in neck-cloths who negotiated in 1814 the Peace of Ghent, and restored to the Anglo-Saxon community in two continents that unaccountable peace which passes all understanding. As diplomacy it is depressingly *bourgeois;* but as an excuse for James Gallatin's first visit to Europe it is admirable. Other excuses were subsequently provided by the State Department, when it made his father Ambassador in France and England; and that astonishing young man, who acted as his secretary, was definitely loose on European society.

James, as his British publisher merrily observed, "was a gay young spark in Paris." Even Lord Bryce expresses the opinion that he was "not so well regulated" as his sister Frances; and the comparison does the young lady every credit. He went to St. Petersburg in 1813, when the Emperor was out of town fighting Napoleon; and he became the shuttle-cock of Anglo-American diplomacy from Russia to Amsterdam, and from Amsterdam to London. James was shocked at the spectacle of Russian alcoholism, but it was nothing to the English Sunday. "English-women are not pretty; they are either coarse or very delicate. Complexions fine, but too red"—young James was seventeen, but he had an eye. "I have seen the Prince Regent walking in the Mall. He is handsome"; James's ideal of male beauty would seem a little Vitellian, and his own appearance fell far below the standard set by H.R.H.: "I wore a suit of Chinese nankin, white silk stockings, high white choker, with a breastpin of seed-pearls mother gave me before I left home. They call my hair auburn—I call it red." James moved on with the American mission to Ghent —"the women are so ugly here"—and did his diplomatic duties.

Then began his real life, which consisted in meeting every one in Europe and making impertinent comments on them. James in his diary was as pert and vivid as one of Mr. Compton Mackenzie's chorus-girls; and the result is one of the most amusing works of minor history that has ever come to light. His tone bears an uncanny resemblance to the American pertness of Master Randolph Miller of Schenectady, as it was observed by the lake at Vevey forty years ago by Mr. Henry James's contemplative young Bostonian. That small boy of nine, with "an aged expression of countenance, a pale complexion, and sharp features," who played the *enfant terrible* in the tragedy of his sister Daisy, has the authentic Gallatin ring. They must often have said of James in the Gallatin family: "He says he doesn't care much about old castles. He's only nine. He wants to stay at the hotel. Mother's afraid to leave him, and the courier won't stay with him; so we haven't been to many places."

His speciality was insolent observation of the European scene. He found Napoleon fat and Madame de Staël "oddly dressed, seeming to have one or two skirts on top of the other." Joseph Bonaparte "acts as if he were still King of Spain"; and Madame Réca-mier "is beautiful, but I could not see great intelligence in her face." He wrote a page of his diary in

161

Voltaire's chair at Ferney and Madame de Staël called him *"Cupidon."* Meanwhile James's father went solemnly about Europe, looking up his ancestors and disapproving of the Bonapartes for being so middle-class. There is an extremely interesting conversation with Napoleon at Elba, in which the Emperor, "suddenly recollecting himself" in the midst of a political discussion, said: *"Mais ce n'est pas mon affaire—je suis mort."* The gesture was borrowed later, consciously or not, by the Empress Eugénie.

Then James reached Paris, and his career began in earnest. David painted him as Cupid; and "I don't think father will approve of my picture." These were the days when Napoleon was marching on Paris with 1,100 men; and James walked about the streets and saw men turning their coats as he went. The Emperor sent for Albert Gallatin, and was distinctly rude to him when he declined to be drawn on the subject of American policy, having evidently forgotten (those Bonapartes were always *bourgeois*) that he was a Swiss aristocrat. And so the diary continues for fourteen years with its delightful blend of personal and political comment. There were so many people in the world in those days; and James's insolent appreciation of his surroundings is refreshingly, boyishly indiscreet. Madame de Boigne, Talleyrand, the Bourbons, the Prince Regent at Brighton, Canning,

and innumerable little ladies hurry through the pages
of this historical Revue; and Albert Gallatin, the
peacemaker, who is the solemn excuse for its preservation, appears from time to time, thinking—like
Lord Burleigh.

SUPERMEN

I. GENTLEMEN ADVENTURERS

King Frederick the Great
King Louis Philippe
Mr. Disraeli, Statesman
Mr. Disraeli, Novelist
Mr. Disraeli, Journalist
Mr. Delane
M. Adolphe Thiers
M. Léon Gambetta
General Walker

KING FREDERICK THE GREAT

SOMEWHERE in the Canon or Apocrypha of Mr. H. G. Wells there are some assorted reflections which might be profitably digested by nearly all historians, as well as by those exceptional and gifted critics of literature who can read as well as write. They deal, in that staccato intellectual shorthand which enables Mr. Wells to keep more balls in the air at one time than any other contemporary conjurer, with what poor Boon called "the creation of countervailing reputations," that queer habit of competitive panegyric to which we owe the strongly Napoleonic flavour of the Hindenburg legend, the Stevensonian glories of Sir James Barrie, and the Gladstonian prestige of Mr. Asquith.

The Western world ripe for Great Men in the early nineteenth century. The Germans as a highly competitive and envious people take the lead. The inflation of Schiller. The greatness of Goethe. . . . Resolve of the Germans to have a Great Fleet, a Great Empire, a Great Man. Difficulty in finding a suitable German for Greatening. Expansion of the Goethe legend. German efficiency brought to bear on the task. Lectures, Professors. Goethe compared to Shakespeare. Compared to Homer. Compared to Christ. Compared to God. Discovered to be incomparable. . . .

Stimulation of Scotch activities. . . . The discovery that Burns was as great as Shakespeare. Greater. The booming of Sir Walter Scott. Wake up, England! . . . Victorian age sets up as a rival to the Augustan. . . . Tennyson as Virgil. . . .

Longfellow essentially an American repartee. . . .

The theory is not so wildly improbable as Mr. Wells's cheerful advocacy might lead an elderly intelligence to believe. Many a sound doctrine has failed to find acceptance because its nervous parent left it on the workhouse steps, or conquered a natural diffidence by launching it upon the world with the defiant air of one about to pull the neighbours' bells and run away. But a solemn world must not be misled by the tone of truculent originality assumed by the author of *The Natural History of Greatness* into dismissing his views with that smile which marks the incurable frivolity of really serious people. Because the truth is sometimes quite amusing, too.

The historian's gallery is full of examples of such competitive imitation. Sometimes the competitor is the man himself; and in such cases he merely presents the spectacle, familiar to fabulists, of the frog stimulated to feats of abnormal distension by the more generous contours of the bull. The eyeglass of Mr.

Austen Chamberlain, and the consciously Napoleonic
gestures of most ordinary persons at any crisis in the
history of their bank, administration, or trade union,
are all instances, more or less distressing, of the same
habit of imitation.

But its more sinister manifestations are those upon
which Mr. Wells has put the unerring finger of the
late Boon. These are the cases in which the imi-
tative colouring is deliberately superimposed by a
third party as a conscious set-off to some existing
reputation. The trick springs partly from that base
commercialism which is for ever thrusting one thing
upon us, whilst pretending all the time that it is
something else. It has poisoned the pure streams
of historical and literary criticism, like a chemical
works fouling a fishery; and even the clear spring of
geography, that virgin science dwelling alone among
the watersheds and wooed only by the geometrical
embraces of Mr. Belloc, has hardly escaped the vile
infection. The habit of mind which can bring men
to speak of the Cornish Riviera, the Saxon Switzerland, and the Manchester of France is an unpleasant evidence of the same device which leads them to
describe Mr. Robert W. Service as the Canadian
Kipling and may yet encourage them to stigmatize
Mr. Kipling as the British D'Annunzio.

One of the most striking instances of this distressing form of propaganda is the organized effort made over a number of years by large portions of the population of North Germany to establish King Frederick the Great as a sort of Prussian repartee to the reputation of the Emperor Napoleon. The history of the Seven Years' War was conscientiously ransacked for parallels to every incident in the Napoleonic mythology. If the Emperor was obstructed by an irreverent sentry, the King of Prussia must needs have been defied by a disrespectful miller. If the Imperial cavalry was habitually commanded by Murat in the most preposterous headgear, Ziethen's hussar cap is dutifully magnified to more than Neapolitan proportions by those patriotic historians who have entered their royal master for this exacting competition with the Corsican ogre. Napoleon's correspondence was published by a Bonaparte in thirty-two volumes: a whole dynasty of Hohenzollerns promptly countered with the re-issue of Frederick in thirty-six. The Frederician *tricorne* was given a Napoleonic tilt; and illustrators who caught him with a royal hand on the shoulders of a Pomeranian grenadier, set his fingers groping Napoleonically upwards for the lobe of his *grognard's* ear. And so the game went on. If Napoleon had taken (which he did not) the faintest interest in the port of Kiel, the *Preussiche Jahrbücher* would doubt-

less have restored the balance by laying down two
Kiels to one. And one positively wonders that no
enterprising graduate of the University of Berlin
ever managed to catch him sleeping before the battle
of Rossbach or marooned him for a short time on an
Elba in the Baltic.

But the significance of Frederick is not in the
least that he was Napoleonic, which he was not. This
lean-faced, elegant little atheist, who swung a censer
before the altar of Voltaire and received extensive
presents of *rococo* clocks from the Pompadour, was
typically a figure of the Eighteenth Century. He
belongs essentially to that period of deportment, in
which the occupation of the statesman was closely
allied to the still higher calling of the dancing-master,
and the differences of nations were adjusted by certain formal movements of small professional armies
resembling almost equally the square dances of the
ballroom and the gentlemanly exercises of the duel-
ling-ground. That is why the point of him is so completely missed in any attempt to run his career into
the larger mould of the post-Revolutionary era,
when governments said what they meant with the most
indelicate emphasis, and whole nations were locked
in strikingly inelegant struggles for their existence.

The value of this little figure of Frederick as
a summary of the whole tone of his century was de-

bated and (at considerable length) exploited by
Carlyle, whose writings are avoided by the present
generation which cannot read Scotsmen, under the
false pretence that he was really a German. The
great tapestry into which he angrily wove that period
in which the continent of Europe was converted into
a large drawing-room, is one of the soundest and
most elaborate pieces of historical research and description ever made.

Just as philosophy is the study of other people's
misconceptions, so history is the study of other people's mistakes. They are mostly the mistakes of
historians, who in their habit of erring are almost
human. There is a popular error with an increasing
circle of popularity to the effect that the Eighteenth
Century was a barren period. It is typical of the
Victorian snobbery of the Nineteenth Century that
it denied its own father because he looked like a
walking gentleman in a costume-play. The illusion
of futility was fostered by the circumstance that
the Eighteenth Century dressed lamentably well and
had deplorably good manners. It was assumed by
solemn gentlemen in black coats that a generation
which could furnish its rooms could not conceivably
furnish its mind; and we were given to understand
that the century of the three Georges was passed in
a genial blend of alcoholism and deportment. It is

an unfortunate impression, because that century laid
the foundation of modern England. It may have
laid them a little gaily, between minuets; but, however light-minded its recreations may have been,
it undoubtedly laid them. Industrialism, economics, and political Radicalism were all produced by
the age of the six-bottle men; and the honest historian is bound to admit that everything that is
modern is eighteenth-century, just as the honest
furniture dealer is driven by his conscience to con-
fess that nearly everything that is eighteenth-century is modern.

The period which was pregnant with the American
Republic and the French Revolution produced the
most modern of all the seven plagues of Europe,
the temper of Prussia. The Eighteenth Century was
the school of all diplomacy; but above all it was the
nursery of Prussian diplomacy. In the month of
August, 1914, when several Prussians were detected
in public untruth, English opinion was directed in its
search for precedents to the writings of an academic
person named Treitschke and a commander of cavalry named Bernhardi. Since the people of England
had been seized with an unusual desire to read something about foreigners, it was perhaps fortunate that
the works of these writers were available in English
translations. But it was hardly the proper place to

look for the origins of Prussian policy, because you do not find the roots of a tree amongst its higher branches. It is not so long since Prussian history began; and there are present in the beginnings of Prussian history all the elements which have recently become familiar. It was the discovery of Horace that there were heroes before Agamemnon; and it remains for some English historian still unborn to reveal to our posterity that there were Germans before Bismarck. Before Nietzsche and Treitschke there was Frederick the Great. He ruled Prussia for half a century, and in a series of three wars he made that country one of the great Powers of Europe. His diplomacy was frankly mendacious; and when in the first year of his reign he got his first opportunity of violating the peace of Europe, he took it in twenty-seven days. It is possibly more instructive to study the proceedings of the greatest King of Prussia than to read the lectures of the innumerable gentlemen of the same nationality who have conceived it to be the duty of a professor to teach the young idea how to shoot upon insufficient provocation.

The whole world outside the charmed circle of Copenhagen and Amsterdam was busily engaged for five years in demonstrating that there is nothing original in Germany except its original sin. The exercise was enjoyable, and since England has always appreciated destructive criticism as a legitimate form of sport, it was extremely popular. Exhuming Goethe was almost as entertaining as killing Keats. It was delightful to observe the antics of philosophers shunning the feet of innumerable Gamaliels; and the musicians have grown as suspicious of their old masters as picture dealers. A Major-General even hinted that the 42-centimetre howitzer was an Austrian invention; and the great Germans all became Swedes or Swiss. But there is one invention to which the Prussian claim has never been denied, and that is the peculiar blend of legitimate ambition with illegitimate methods which is known as *Realpolitik*. The original specification is probably to be found among the papers of an Italian author of quotations named Macchiavelli. Professor Chamberlain, whose popularity has somewhat unaccountably waned in this country, has probably demonstrated that this so-called Florentine had a thick neck and butter-coloured hair; perhaps his Tuscan was a shade guttural. At any rate, even if Macchiavelli was not himself of pronouncedly Teutonic type, his ingenious invention has received in North Germany such substantial additions that it has definitely become a Prussian patent. Frederick or Bismarck could probably defend with complete success any patent action that the misguided Italian might bring against them.

Realpolitik is in reality the diplomacy of the Eighteenth Century; it belongs to the period before nationalism had arisen to prohibit partitions, and when preventive wars were the common exercise of nations. Modern diplomacy is a good way behind its times. Among Englishmen it has just reached the vague nationalism which pervaded Europe between 1848 and the collapse of the Second Empire; but in Prussia it belongs purely to the Eighteenth Century. The invasion of Belgium was purely Frederician; the Turkish alliance was the normal expedient of the ministers of Louis XV; and Dr. von Bethmann-Hollweg could have opened his heart to Kaunitz.

Prussian policy entered European history with the suddenness of a bad fairy in the late autumn of 1740, when Frederick became King of Prussia. That young man ascended the throne with the most sinister of all reputations, a name for bad verse. Politically he appeared to be an enlightened pacifist with a strong moral bias against Macchiavelli. But promotion, which was powerless to improve his verse, debased his morals; and in the first year of his reign, within four weeks of his first opportunity, he committed a European crime. He invaded Silesia in direct contravention of the written guarantee of his Government. Since he was a humorist and had excellent manners, he offered to protect his victim against any other criminal whom he might meet; and for the next forty-six years Prussian policy was conducted on the lines laid down by the best contemporary highwayman. Various coaches were stopped, with assistance of various allies, and it was occasionally convenient to turn king's evidence. An English writer has referred to his "royal Larkinism"; but he was surely confusing Mr. James Larkin with Mr. Richard Turpin.

The *amateur* of Frederick will find little to revise in his old Carlylean impression of the European scene and the Prussian actors in it. Once more, as in the more familiar case of Gibbon, the imagination of genius would appear to have anticipated the conclusions of research; and the utmost that industrious young men can achieve to-day in the archives of Berlin and Vienna is to confirm the conjectures of an irritable old man in Chelsea in the early Sixties. Perhaps one of them will one day produce a study of Frederick William I, the Philip of this *rococo* Alexander, whose achievement in the direction of Prussian policy and the construction of a Prussian army was infinitely more valuable than the more advertised career of his predecessor, the Great Elector, and was at least as important for Germany and Europe as the work which Frederick himself was enabled to do on the foundations that his father had laid.

177

But one is always glad to read books about Frederick, if only for the memories which they revive. There are some books which set a man groping blindly up the dusty corridors of his intellectual past; and with the belated study of a life of Frederick the Great one almost recovers—it is a gorgeous sensation—the fine frenzy of the Early Days, of those autumn evenings in 1914 when one used to read the *communiqués* (how strange the word looked!) of a Mr. F. E. Smith not yet ennobled, upon the operations of a Sir John French not yet enshrined. In those days the country, which had embarked in August on a war of honour and policy, found itself by the exigencies of the autumn publishing season engaged in a war of ideas; and the pens of England were levelled in a thin, black line at the oncoming squadrons of iniquity led by the sinister trinity of Nietzsche, Treitschke, and Bernhardi. Someone even made quite a lot of money by blandly republishing those chapters of *The Decline and Fall* which relate to the unsuccessful enterprise of Attila; and the public intelligence was rotten-ripe to receive revelations of the cynical depravity of Frederick the Great. But none came.

It was notorious to any leader-writer with the strength to quote Macaulay's essay that he had invaded Silesia without extenuating circumstances (the

foolish man did not even realize the mining prospects
of the region) ; and it was very generally felt that he
was in some way the father of the Prussian evil, in
spite of the distressing fact that British policy had
rendered every assistance to this disreputable paternity. Yet nervous propagandists quailed before the
backs of Carlyle's six (or, in some editions, eight)
volumes, and the Iliad of Frederician naughtiness remained unsung.

But it is an unfortunate irony that has delayed
the publication of any new biography of Frederick
until the iron, which the historian might have struck
when it was so beautifully hot, is already cooling in
the air of a less fevered day. The ambitious biographer, as a more gifted writer might say in a City column, is caught a bear of Hohenzollerns; in the
Miscellaneous Market Huns are rather a languid feature (what a gift they have in Throgmorton Street
for rich, pictorial metaphor!), and Attila closed soft.

That is why it seems rather a pity that a brilliant
young man is upon us, nearly twelve months after
the closing of the Ministry of Information, with the
discovery that "Frederick's military reputation was
in excess of his deserts, owing to misrepresentations
made by himself or by others on his behalf. . . . He
lived in a chronic state of premature despair . . .
and indulged freely in tears . . . on the battlefield he

179

gave several exhibitions of cowardice . . . he ordered
the refusal of quarter, treated prisoners and wounded
with inhumanity, bombarded cathedrals and cut down
fruit trees: and received from his contemporaries the
name of the 'Attila of the North.' "

This has the ripe, authentic tang of the vintage
of 1914. One hangs breathlessly on the historian's
lips to hear the tale of how Frederick flung a sneer
at Maria Theresa's "contemptible little army," ordered his submarine commanders to sink the Saxon
food-ships at sight, and sent Montgolfiers to drop
grenades on the most populous portions of Vienna.
Instead, one finds only rather tittering anecdotes
about his bad style, his aversion for washing, and his
neglect to shave.

It was not easy for a son to survive the paternity
of Frederick William I; but he achieved it. It was
not simple to fight the Prussian corner through the
Seven Years' War, to stand up against Russia,
France, and Austria with no more substantial ally
than British sea-power, of which no Admiral Mahan
had yet explained the sovereign qualities to an obedi-
ent world; but he managed it, living, as they say, from
hand to mouth—and if, as his biographers delight to
tell us, it was sometimes a shaking hand and a wry
mouth, one is not really so very surprised. It was
not child's play to recreate Prussia into a position of

European significance after the war was won: the reconstruction of victorious countries has since that day been worse done by better men than Frederick. But his biographers show a singular lack of interest in the administrative achievement of the twenty years of peace which form the second and less dramatic chapter of his reign. It is a pity, because Frederick was never more the Hohenzollern in his versatility or more the German in his thoroughness. But perhaps our historians feel that he was not quite sufficiently the Hun.

The final interest of the Frederician *épopée* lies in the fact that the king was the fine flower of European monarchy in its later form. Kingship, which had resulted in the first instance from the hero-worship of primitive times, waned like a candle in the dawn before the fierce sunlight of the later Reformation. The units which composed the European state-system became too large in the early Seventeenth Century to be manipulated by a single pair of hands. The increasing complexity of the world dictated the relegation of important duties to mere ministers at the same time as philosophers were beginning to feel what Mr. Max Beerbohm has called "a horrid doubt as to the Divine Right." But in a final effort monarchy returned upon Europe in a new form. If the king could not be the tallest, the strongest, or the richest man in his kingdom, he would at least be socially supreme. The thing began with the unamiable posturings of Louis XIV, and radiated from Versailles through the Western World. It was perhaps typical of the age of deportment that it expressed its veneration of its masters in the niceties of etiquette rather than by the clashing of sword-blades upon shields. Such was the seed-bed which produced the revival of kingship in the middle Eighteenth Century, when France, Russia, Prussia, Austria, Spain, Portugal, Naples, Piedmont, and Tuscany slowly pirouetted, each to the tune of its single dynast, and even England stumbled into the measure played by King George III. Of this time and temper Frederick is almost the most typical product. His intellectual *liaison* with Voltaire ranked him with that crowned *Intelligentzia* of which the Empress Catherine was the most entertaining and the Emperor Joseph the most industrious member; and that blend of absolutism and enlightenment, which led him to gratify a passion for administrative detail in the intervals of playing on the flute and composing Alexandrine verse, was characteristic to the last degree.

He reigned for forty-six years; and when he died, the storm of the Bastille was only three years distant, and men must almost have heard the sound of the tumbrils coming up the wind. There was not a king left in Europe to hold the pass for Kingship. The fumbling intellectualism of Austria, the dullness of that heavy man, France, Prussia with his mystics and his bigamy, England's alternations of rusticity and mental collapse, Naples who kept an eating-house *incognito,* the stupid Spain who offered himself to the pictorial obloquy of Goya and never noticed the caricature—these were hardly the men to stand up against the burning wind that swept from the Place de la Révolution across Europe. For the last of the kings had died in a room at Potsdam.

KING LOUIS PHILIPPE

WHEN an inquiring posterity reads Tono-Bungay (or "The Swiss Family Whittaker") in order to see how Mr. H. G. Wells found his way about one of Mr. Arnold Bennett's hotels, it will discover, as one generally does, an extremely interesting passage about something else. Mr. Edward Ponderevo, whose bankruptcy proceedings were initiated in order to discover under which particular thimble the pea was at that moment secreted and subsequently became a leading case because it was found that there was no pea, was at one moment of his career an ardent Napoleonist. He collected, as we are told, the more convex portraits of the great artillerist, and was frequently observed to stand in profile against windows with the hand of Montenotte thrust into the waistcoat of Wagram about as far up as the knuckles of Aspern-Essling. Now a Napoleonist, as any antique-dealer will tell you, is a thing totally distinct from a Bonapartist. Bonapartists are persons of simple faith (but not necessarily Norman blood), whose loyalty has survived successive transfers to a slack-minded Romantic with a Spanish wife, an anæmic young gentleman at Sandhurst, and a commissioned officer in the Russian army. They preach the remarkable doctrine of salvation by plébiscite, and they believe, as the late President Lincoln so justly and so nearly remarked, in government by the Eagle for the Eagle.

But the Napoleonist is a far more complex and dangerous phenomenon. He collects things. They may be discarded epaulettes, spent bullets from the Moscow campaign, or the theses of American professors: but if they are connected in any particular with the *Grande Armée,* he acquires them with the silent persistence of those old gentlemen in Henry James who accumulated florid Continental furniture with the impeccably bad taste of nineteenth-century culture. When the bridges were breaking at the Beresina, his ancestor was probably running up and down the bank looking for splinters to preserve as relics. He has, so to say, the Bees in his bonnet; and if he were asked suddenly for his name by the catechist, he would probably reply that it was N with a little crown on top. That is precisely what happened to Mr. Ponderevo.

This fancied resemblance to great men is one of

the oddest tricks of human imagination. It resides
originally in the desire of a person to add a syllable
to his stature and become a personage. There was
an imbecile King of Naples (there were several) who
humped his shoulder and twisted his neck on parade
and even cultivated that hunted eye which comes from
spending seven years on the road between one's Eastern and one's Western fronts, in order solely to look
like Frederick the Great. The oddest thing about the
sedulous ape is that he always selects for imitation
those characters whose value is more meretricious
than substantial. One knows scores of City men who
thought that they were like Mr. Chamberlain; but
there is no recorded instance of a stockbroker with
a fancied resemblance to Lord Shaftesbury. It is the
tragedy of French history that it has produced several
people who thought they were like Napoleon, and
nobody who thought he was like Louis Philippe: it
is a pity. A resemblance to Napoleon made a failure
of *Plon-Plon,* and remained a comparatively blind-
alley occupation until the advent of the cinematograph afforded a crowded and competitive avenue
of employment. But a resemblance to Louis Philippe is a guarantee of a sound and serviceable article, suitable for domestic use. He was the sort of
monarch who is useful about the house. Sometimes
he was more than a trifle suburban: that is where the

186

Napoleon of Peace comes nearest to the Napoleon of Notting Hill.

Louis Philippe, if one may draw up for a moment before that neglected career like an erratic train before a deserted halt, is one of the few successes that give all the impression of failure. He was an *arriviste* who arrived; but one never realizes it. Like Napoleon he died in exile; and like General Seely he saved life from drowning. But somehow one never sees him set with that splendid company on the high and windy stage of fame. He was once a teacher of geography, which brings him near to Mr. Belloc; and he reconstructed the Palace of Versailles, which reminds one of Louis XIV. He filled several caricatures by Daumier; and he was at one time Mr. Disraeli's ideal of regal deportment. But one feels that he will never figure in a symbolical picture by Mr. Goetze or be impersonated by Mr. Dennis Eadie. Perhaps it is because of his undoubted family virtues, or because his *floruit* was *circa* 1840, or because he omitted to shave the sides of his face. But in spite of his pictorial disadvantages, which must have been acutely present to the mind of a romantic novelist, his biography was once written, if not by the hand, at least in the *atelier* of Dumas. When a pusillanimous executive endeavoured to raise revenue by imposing a tax on *feuilletons,* the managing director

of the syndicate that traded in the name of Dumas
père was not to be defeated by this dastardly attempt
to increase his cost of production. He abandoned the
feuilleton, substituted popular history for popular
fiction, and produced tax-free studies of Louis XIV,
Louis XV, and Louis Philippe. Dumas was always
a trifle ridiculous when he was political; and his history has a strong flavour of his incredible address to
the electors of the Yonne: "Citizens, I am the son
of the Republican General, Alexandre Dumas, one
of the most admirable children of the first Revolution;
I am the author of *The Three Musketeers,* that is to
say, one of the most national books, both in matter
and colouring, which our literature contains. Thus
introduced, I solicit your support as representative
of the Department of the Yonne." His tone and attitude were always a trifle reminiscent of the comic
Frenchman in a British play produced during a
period of acute Gallophobia; and as the biographer of
Louis Philippe he sometimes found it necessary to
insert in that career the flourishes which his subject
had inartistically omitted.

The King of the French, like so many heroes of
romance, was somewhat unfortunate in his father.
His parentage was even doubted by a lady called
Maria Stella Petronilla, who lived in the Apennines
and maintained heroically, in face of all the circum-

stances, that he was really a girl. One is reminded of those indomitable controversialists who are always comforted by the conviction that Queen Elizabeth was really a red-headed village boy. In the years which separated the American from the French Revolution he lived a life of juvenile elegance, until the movement of fashion was suspended by the birth of a nation, as a Mr. Griffith has taught us to call something far less important which is believed to have taken place subsequently on the Temperance side of the Atlantic. There was a peasant insurrection in France, an urban Revolution in Paris, and a clerical rising in the Austrian Netherlands, which an unwary translator or an unskilled workman on Dumas' night-shift has described as "this insurrection of the Austrians against the Belgians." The Duke of Orleans arrived, in anticipation of the Emperor Napoleon, at the conviction that God is on the side of the big battalions; and deciding that there were more French subjects than French Bourbons, he joined, in the electioneering sense, the great majority. His son wrote a letter to Marat's newspaper and became usher of the Jacobins' Club. There was a man of the name of Robespierre who wore striped waistcoats and looked after the Strangers' Gallery; and it was the privilege of the young gentleman who was to be King of the French to call for

189

silence for almost all the men of the Revolution. In the year 1791 one could be elegant about the regeneration of humanity. He wrote gracefully to Madame de Genlis: "The two things I care most for in all the world are the new Constitution and you." But as the Revolution dropped to a deeper note, it became less easy for a prince to include it in his range. The young Louis Philippe, in an effort to retain his loyalty, became military and went to Metz with Kellermann. Dumas does unexpected justice to the reputation of Dumouriez; and Valmy, where Louis Philippe commanded a division under Kellermann, is accurately described except for the insertion of an infantry contact which never happened. But a novelist could no more tolerate a battle which was won because the weather was wet and the Prussians had eaten sour grapes than Victor Hugo could resist the sunk road of Ohain, when he flashed the battle of Waterloo on to the screen in the later stages of *Les Misèrables*. Seven months later the desertion of Dumouriez carried the young man across the Belgian frontier; and Louis Philippe, who in many ways resembled the hero of the Odyssey, began in the neighbourhood of Mons the long wandering that was to end in the drawing-room Monarchy of July. He assumed, with a foreigner's incapacity to form a serious English name, the egregious appellation of

"Mr. Corby," and eventually sailed from Hamburg for the United States. The King of the French shares with Louis Napoleon and the King of Westphalia the distinction of an American *Wanderjahr;* Jerome and Louis Philippe passed from Poughkeepsie to a throne. It is a singular career; and only the active intervention of the French people in the year 1848 secured that it was not plural.

MR. DISRAELI, STATESMAN

WITH the education of contemporary taste, the resemblance of Lord Beaconsfield to Mr. Mantalini is becoming noticeable, even to members of the Primrose League. The Suez Canal shares show a comfortable profit of nine hundred per cent.; the Treaty of Berlin has not yet been seen through by more than half the population of the Balkan Peninsula; and a living dramatist has approached the theme if not with the Nelson, at least with the Parker touch. But there is a regrettable and increasing tendency on the part of posterity to be irreverent about a statesman who appears to have borrowed his *haute politique* from Mr. William Le Queux, and his *haute finance* from the *New Witness*. One feels, in the cold light of this sweeter, simpler reign, that there is a faintly disreputable air of Early Victorian raffishness about that singular career. There is something the matter with his period. One may respect almost any *Zeitgeist,* if only it will not wear ridiculous clothes. But when it comes with its head wreathed in wax flowers and its hands full of scraps of *papier-mâché*, casting mother of pearl before swine, enthusiasms are apt to grow a trifle faint; and even collectors of *bric-à-brac* turn sadly in other directions. Which is the worst of the Great Victorians.

The broad outline of Disraeli's career is respectable, and even distinguished; but its detail is appalling. That is why the call of the multiple watch-chain is growing fainter, and the visual appeal of bottle-green trousering is beginning to fail across the grey distances of the North Temperate Zone. The fatal elegance of that *coiffure* has shocked a generation which prefers its heroes bald; and it is not easy to respect a statesman who habitually thought of the upper classes like an upper servant. In his *Life* one is perpetually overhearing asides which sound less like the confessions of an ex-Minister than the comments of a retired, if slightly cynical, butler. But for all that, it was a great career informed by a magnificent, if inaccurate, imagination. For Disraeli, whether in his novels or his politics, dukes were perpetually coming down to breakfast in full Garter robes, whilst the ancestral standard was run up on the Norman keep and a brass band crashed out the National Anthem in the dining-room. It may be, as his biographer ruefully remarks of his gusto at the wedding of Queen Alexandra, that "the trappings of

royal and noble life appealed to his sense of fitness."
But at least they are more inspiring than the bleak
broad-cloth of Mrs. Humphry Ward; and as Disraeli
conceived his career as a show, it is gratifying that
the Beaconsfield Trustees have found him a biographer who would not give the show away.

Disraeli's reputation, as the American said of the
British Empire, is "a queer, queer thing." It is not
easy to recover the first rapture with which the Victorians received the miracle of a politician who could
both write and speak, or to disinter from maiden
hearts the ineffable romance of a Chancellor of the
Exchequer who wrote fiction. To the modern eye
those ringlets are almost lack-lustre; and the figure,
that fascinated Queen Victoria, as it posed in Oriental attitudes against the tartan wall-paper of Os-
borne, has lost something of its power. The emerald
trousers and the canary-coloured waistcoat, which
drew the early Forties as with a magnet, fail somehow in their grip upon an age which dresses badly,
but with some method in its badness; and there is
little romance in the feeling for aristocracy which
Disraeli shared with Miss Marie Corelli. The East
is full of mysteries, even after *Kismet* and Mr. Robert Hichens. But it is least mysterious when its
waistcoat is full of watch-chains; *ex oriente nux* is
a familiar and an unattractive emblem. Yet it is pos-

sible in the cold dawn of the present century to forget Disraeli's fantastic parades across proud and peacock- haunted parterres, and to estimate his true value and business in English politics. Although it is a figure which appeals irresistibly to the undergraduate imagination with its suggestion of a belated D'Orsay or a premature Randolph Churchill, it is a career with a more serious value for politicians. Disraeli was to some extent the Treitschke of British Imperialism; and on the side of party politics he produced a strain of Toryism which approached almost to the possession of ideas. It may be true that those ideas were either Radical or wrong; but it was a unique achievement to have brought the Country party within thinking range of anything. It results that Disraeli's politics have become the favourite study of rising young men; his observations are quoted, with or without acknowledgment, in the common-rooms of our great universities; and his name was applauded in some of the larger music-halls up to within a few months of the war. There can be little doubt that the gradual publication of his official biography contributed something to this revival; and it is for modern criticism to ascertain whether it is a revival of the fittest.

It has been observed that statesmen get the biographers that they deserve: that is where posterity hits back. There is something delightfully suitable about the final biography of Disraeli. Its subject spent years in the endeavour to convert himself from a *bizarre* and romantic Bedouin into an elderly English aristocrat with ideas; and he would rejoice in the solemn and uninspired pages in which he is now presented to posterity. The biography is final, painstaking, and complete; and the whole thing is rather like *The Times* before it became *autre temps*. It lacks the light touch of Disraelian impertinence; but monuments of this class are apt to be more perennial than brass, if less amusing. Disraeli's career is made to appear not so much startling as inevitable, as he moves (like one of Mr. Gladstone's perorations) "to a not far distant goal"; and Mr. Buckle, from his praise of his predecessor to his acknowledgments to Lord Rothschild and the King, commits no single error of taste or discretion: it is, in a biographer, a great omission.

Disraeli early emerged from the exotic chrysalis with which he had scandalized Victorian society, and settled soberly into English politics. So early as the year 1852 he was painted by the President of the Royal Academy in a complete black outfit; he was even wearing a black tie. His judicious marriage placed him beyond the need of money, and he moved easily up and down the pages of Debrett; in the year 1846 he sat at table with four lords and a duke.

It was in the days after the repeal of the Corn Laws, when Disraeli had tomahawked Peel out of office, that he began to loom large in the political world of loaves and fish-dinners at Greenwich and to acquire a serious position in the Tory Party. The leadership of the Protectionists was in that state of eclipse which has since become its tradition. Lord George Bentinck was an extremely worthy man; but when his biographer observes that Disraeli "was much tried by the behaviour of his leader, who discredited himself by a number of petty personal charges of jobs and blunders against Peel's late Government," and adds that "the charges were all satisfactorily repelled," one marvels at the continuity of the Tory tradition. In the following year Disraeli moved forward to the Front Bench, and transferred his membership from Shrewsbury to High Wycombe; it was the beginning of his advance. When the question of the leadership was raised on Bentinck's death, the Country party was faced with the unfortunate necessity of choosing a spokesman who was un-English, but intelligent. Disraeli had made a militant demonstration of his Hebraism in the publication of *Tancred*. Like many Jews who have forsaken their religion, he was doubly emphatic as to his race; and his description of the Church as "a sacred corporation for the promulgation and maintenance in Europe of certain Asian principles" must have petrified the bishops as surely as it would convert Mr. Belloc into a stream of molten lava. In the result he cut his party clear of Protection and led them back into office, in spite of the fact that Prince Albert felt "very uneasy" as to the laxity of his political conscience.

He approached the year 1848 with a veneration for "the serene intelligence of the profound Metternich" and a regard for Louis Philippe that was almost filial; and it is hardly surprising that a year that left "the King of France in a Surrey villa, Metternich in a Hanover Square Hotel, and the Prince of Prussia at Lady Palmerston's" found him slightly shocked. Disraeli informed the House of Commons that Louis Philippe had succeeded "in riding for a period of seventeen years the Jacobin tiger," and omitted to notice that on his return from the excursion the aged monarch had exactly followed the precedent of the young lady of Riga. But Disraeli rarely joked about royalty, from these early days until he made his astonished Queen into an Oriental potentate, and left the stage in a blaze of shooting Stars and revolving Garters.

Disraeli was generally in Opposition in the company of a number of frivolous old gentlemen known as the Tory Party. Opposition came as natural to Disraeli as Reform Bills to Lord John Russell; and he is, perhaps, the only man since Charles Fox whose intellect has survived a protracted residence on the left of the Speaker without deteriorating into what we have learnt euphemistically to describe as "ginger." His Oppositions opposed; but they were rarely ridiculous and sometimes constructive. In the year 1855 his country was at war with Russia for some reason of which the secret was admirably kept by the Foreign Office; and the people of England called, in accordance with their practice on these occasions, for a Man. This flattering appellation was first fixed upon Lord Derby; but the fourteenth Earl was disinclined to anticipate his descendant in this virile character, and he took no steps, apart from a speech which Lord Henry Lennox described, with an uncanny prevision of Mr. Shaw, as "the old roar of the British Lion." The demand for a dictator was finally satisfied by an elderly Irish peer with a remarkable instinct for the requirements of the average man; and Lord Palmerston went into office on the shoulders of "majorities collected God knows how, voting God knows why." Disraeli, with a clever man's utter failure to understand unreason, was extremely angry; he pursued his country's choice with

such invective as "an old painted pantaloon," and
"a sort of Parliamentary grandpapa," and even at-
tacked his principles as the manœuvres of "a gay
old Tory of the older school disguising himself as
a Liberal." But he had the intelligence to observe
that "a war Opposition and a war Ministry could
not co-exist": it is a discovery which Mr. Pringle was
one day to share with Mr. Billing.

Meanwhile the Crimean War, which was siege warfare in truth and in fact, went placidly on by the
waters of the Black Sea. Italy came in, in her odd
way; and Disraeli startled an old lady by imparting
to her the alarming figures of national expenditure:

> The war expenditure of France is one million and a half
> sterling per week—that of England one million and a
> quarter! This is a large sum for distant objects and some-
> what equivocal success.

If the old lady would call round again, we could
show her the same article in a more expensive style.
The queer littleness of the Crimea is well illustrated
by another letter, in which Disraeli almost shrieks
that:

> Lady Londonderry is in despair about her son, Lord
> Adolphus Vane, who is now in the trenches. The trenches
> are so near the enemy that we lose forty *per diem* by casual-
> ties. *Casualties*, she says, and truly, what a horrible word
> to describe the loss of limb and life!

"They order, said I, this matter better in France."

But the war brought its compensations for an aspiring member of the Opposition:

> We had the honour of a royal invitation to some of the festivities, and, when I was presented, Napoleon came forward, and shook hands with me cordially, and spoke some gracious words. Our Queen was on his right, the Empress next to her—Prince Albert on the left of the Emperor, then Duchess of Kent, and Duchess of Cambridge and Princess Mary. So one had to make seven reverences.

It really makes one quite giddy, and sounds rather like paying one's respects to a steel engraving.

Two years later, when polite society was intrigued by the appearance of a comet and the usual announcement of the approaching end of the age, the native troops went out at Meerut, and the Victorians were confronted by the inelegant circumstance of the Indian Mutiny. British opinion was unable to grasp the military problem of its suppression; but the atrocities enjoyed a tremendous vogue. Disraeli, who was constitutionally sceptical in such matters, was unable to share the gusto with which his countrymen peered down the Well of Cawnpore:

> The detail of all these stories is suspicious. Details are a feature of the Myth. The accounts are too graphic—I hate the word. Who can have seen these things? Who heard them? The rows of ladies standing with their babies in their arms to be massacred, with the elder children clutch-

ing to their robes—who that could tell these things could have escaped?

This is not such stuff as Bryce Reports are made of. But it serves neatly to indicate the temper of kindly tolerance with which twenty years later Disraeli bore the depopulation of Bulgaria and drove the more sensitive imagination of Mr. Gladstone into the arms of the Little Father.

He developed in these years an astonishing project for the reform of the Civil Service. Failing completely to recognize that the administrative salvation of England is to be sought in the exclusion from public employment of all persons resident in the Borough of Kensington, he contented himself with reconstituting the Departments. The scheme secured the maximum of confusion by combining the War, Marine, and Ordnance Departments in a single ministry; the Post Office was merged in the Treasury; and the Prime Minister became President of the Council, Chancellor of the Duchy of Lancaster, and Lord Privy Seal. There was also to be a Ministry of Poor Laws. Lord Stanley informed his father that "there is no great harm in making one man, the Minister of Poor Laws, a rather more important personage than he need be"; it would have been a graceful prevision of Mr. and Mrs. Webb if he had made it a lady and a gentleman.

Meanwhile the Sixties continued in that atmosphere of commercial prosperity that is so profoundly irritating to Continental observers. Prince Albert died, and Disraeli compared him to Sir Philip Sidney. Count Bismarck emerged, and Disraeli compared him to Cardinal Alberoni. Lord Derby left him the Premiership, and Disraeli compared it to the top of a greasy pole. The invasion of Schleswig-Holstein filled him with ingenious arguments for non-intervention; the manipulation of Luxemburg inspired him with a fear that France and Prussia would treat the Treaty of 1839 in the traditional manner:

Our people might let it be known at Berlin and Paris that the violation of Belgian neutrality should not pass with impunity.

A movement of Irish-Americans (*autres temps, autres* hyphens) provoked a remarkable exposition of Imperial policy:

Leave the Canadians to defend themselves; recall the African squadron; give up the settlements on the west coast of Africa; and we shall make a saving which will, at the same time, enable us to build ships and have a good Budget.

It is a queer programme for the putative father of Imperialism. But there are some odd corners in the edifice of that singular career, which began in the *rococo* and ended in the Flamboyant Gothic. Disraeli's taste for colonies was always apt to break down when it came to colonials; and his principles amounted to little beyond an æsthetic desire to retain India for its decorative qualities. If it was a fault, it was a fault of the imagination. But perhaps it has as much value as the helter-spelter Imperialism of Mr. Hughes.

MR. DISRAELI, NOVELIST

WHEN a distressed posterity enquires why it must look to a man who wore bottle-green trousers and far, far too many watch-chains, for the richest picture of English society in that brilliant period which intervened between the divorce of Queen Caroline and the motherhood of Queen Victoria, the reply must be that after all it takes something of an outsider to be really romantic about English society. For it is only from the outside that any great institution, whether it is a Gothic cathedral, a Government Department, or a London club, can be really impressive. Nothing is sacred to the initiated. No valet, as it has been wisely said, is a hero to his master. Dukes hold no mysteries for duchesses, and baronets seem scarcely wicked to their wives.

That is why there has always been something a trifle exotic, if the language of the hot-house may be applied without ineptitude to Mrs. Humphry Ward, about the literary appreciators of the great world. It is by a similar irony that the nostalgia

205

of Sussex, that chosen home-land of persons who do not belong there, appears to have affected most strongly among their contemporaries Mr. Kipling, who is Anglo-Indian, and Mr. Belloc, who is Anglo-Gallic. But one need not have week-ended with the Merlins in order to write a good account of Broceliaunde. Indeed it would almost seem from the record of English social fiction as though it were only from outside the charmed circle that one can get a really good view of the incantations.

Disraeli, who delighted to see in the British country-house an Olympian resting-place of semi-divine personages between the exercises of the Palæstra and the subtleties of the Senate (how one catches the flavour), was born in Theobald's Road. Du Maurier, who is for ever ushering us into a drawing-room that culminates in the tiara of a Duchess at the end of a long avenue of athletic bishops and majestic peeresses, was more than half a Frenchman and lived at the top of Heath Street. And Henry James, who saw unutterable depths of significance behind the stolid mask of British society, spent half a life-time in the endeavour to forget that he was American-born. So scattered and so queer are the origins of those who have found in Mayfair their spiritual home.

But romance came natural to a young man who first put an author's pen to a publisher's paper in the year 1825. George IV, ignorant of the fatal but posthumous fascination which he was to exercise on Mr. Max Beerbohm, was king; and Stephenson was fumbling laboriously towards a type of locomotive which should resemble a trifle less acutely that kettle which had been his earliest inspiration. But Napoleon was only four years dead, Byron had two years to live, and it was the authentic age of romance. If the moon shone then, you may be sure that it shone fitfully, through ragged clouds, and to an accompaniment of hooting owls upon a world populated almost exclusively by youthful knights and aged abbots. That is the right, the true romance. But the young Disraeli sought it elsewhere. Lytton looked for it always among the last of a species—the Last of the Barons, the Last of the Romans, the Last Days of Pompeii. But Disraeli characteristically found it among the first families in England and the highest in the land. He introduced to the astonished country of his adoption the high romance of the upper classes.

The discovery was announced in a publication which he subsequently stigmatized as "a kind of literary lusus" with that free play of Latinity which is habitual to those whose facility in the dead languages has not been arrested by a classical education; and from the first page of *Vivian Grey* to the last page of *Endymion* he continued to work that richest of all mines, the respect of the Anglo-Saxon for his betters.

He worked it, if one may say so, with *panache*. His magnates lived in greater pomp, his peeresses moved with more exuberant circumstance than those of any rival practitioner. Who can forget that perfect scene "in the morning-room of Brentham"? The Duchess was there, of course; one forgets the title, but surely it is enough to remember that "the Duchess, one of the greatest heiresses of Britain, singularly beautiful and gifted with native grace, had married in her teens one of the wealthiest and most powerful of our nobles, and scarcely older than herself." Is that enough to set the tone?

. . . in the morning-room of Brentham, where the mistress of the mansion sate surrounded by her daughters, all occupied with various works. One knitted a purse, another adorned a slipper, a third emblazoned a page. Beautiful forms in counsel leant over frames glowing with embroidery, while two fair sisters, more remote, occasionally burst into melody, as they tried the passages of a new air, which had been communicated to them in the manuscript of some devoted friend.

That, as an inelegant later age delights to say, is indubitably the stuff, the whole stuff, and nothing but the stuff to give them; and the man who wrote those burning words was, when he wrote them, an ex-

Chancellor of the Exchequer. Could Mr. Bonar Law do as much?

It was a rich, warm night at the beginning of August, when a gentleman enveloped in a cloak, for he was in evening dress, emerged from a club house at the top of St. James' Street and descended that celebrated eminence.

When Mr. Chamberlain gives us the novel which we have so long looked for, one wonders wistfully whether it will begin quite like that.

It is in the tone of these passages that Disraeli pitched the whole of his marvellous tale. His Earls were sometimes Dukes and sometimes Marquises; and once or twice (for the English dearly love a Laud) they were high ecclesiastics. But the scene was always set with alabaster and plush curtains; and the gas-jets were turned high to screaming point, as the flunkeys lined up along the walls and the house-party swept past on its way down to dinner—two Dukes, a Premier, and the Mingrelian Ambassador—and you marvelled, as they went by, to see how easily Mr. Disraeli mingled with this exalted company. That was the fare with which the heated social imagination of this young man provided his countrymen; and it is at least more satisfying than the half-hearted snobbery of his later competitors. Mrs. Humphry Ward's Dukes take off their white kid gloves to begin dinner: Disraeli's draw them on.

But the social picture was not Disraeli's sole asset. There were his wit, his wisdom, his incredible verbal felicity besides. Fifty years before Wilde's young men were born, he was making all their dandy jokes in the intervals of leading the Opposition, and when he sat down for a little recreation after the General Election of 1880, that old, defeated, weary man with the fallen cheeks and the dyed forelock sent up *Endymion* in three volumes of such fireworks as had not been seen since young Mr. D'Israeli first came upon the Town. But it is from his demerits that Disraeli derives his principal value as a Victorian antique. Just as the collector of curios *fin de siècle* now loves to surround himself with the wrong shapes, the bad colouring, the indefensible taste of the objects which disgraced his grandmother's drawing-room, so there is for the collector a wild splendour, a distorted magnificence, an unattractive beauty about Disraeli's social scene. He is a genuine antique, and as such he has a value.

MR. DISRAELI, JOURNALIST

SHORTLY before Mr. Disraeli became Young England's Darling, and many years before his interesting discovery of the British Empire, it was his fortune to contribute to the *Morning Post* and *Times* newspapers a number of political articles. Many men have done worse. He made Tory points in the decade following the Reform Act, 1832, and so far attracted attention that "Fitzgerald says they drank my health in a bumper at Sir H. Hardinge's on Saturday, and said, 'He is the man.'" That was nearly eighty years ago, and the Primrose League was still half a century away. The articles fulfilled their object to the extent of securing for Disraeli the aristocratic patronage of Lord Lyndhurst; and the heroic journalist was enabled to die nightly in last ditches provided for him by the noble lord.

A pious industry has reverently collected these pieces and clothed them in a sober habit uniform with the volumes of the *Life*. Their collection is a characteristically modern enterprise. The note of the times (if they have anything so subdued as a note) is collecting. In an age when men cultivate the congregation of boot-jacks, door-knockers, and spittoons, it is not surprising if the wilder project of collecting newspaper articles finds its adherents. Journalism is of its essence ephemeral. But so are snuff-boxes; and at a time when men accumulate pistols that have lost their locks and clocks that have lost their works, it is hardly surprising if some bolder spirit collects jokes that have lost their points. That, apart from its admitted historical value, is the somewhat dismal atmosphere of the collection. It has the stale flavour of old election addresses. But for the Disraelian its value is considerable. The historical utility of these lost leaders for the clear presentation of the discomfited Toryism of 1836 is respectable. And the industry, with which an editor has made the discovery that Disraeli made the same joke once a year for three years, deserves the fullest credit.

To say truth, Disraeli's journalism is rather portentous stuff. The solemn personalities of his Open Letters, the Ciceronian march of his antitheses, and the majestic procession of a style which referred to O'Connell as "the vagabond delegate of a foreign priesthood" leave one with a feeling of amused awe. But embedded in the bombast of it all there are some astonishingly brilliant phrases: one feels that if only Disraeli would not talk so loud, we might hear some good things. The recurring description of Melbourne's leisured conduct in office ("you might saunter away the remaining years of your now ludicrous existence, sipping the last novel of Paul de Kock, while lounging over a sundial"); the picture of Palmerston ("the Great Apollo of aspiring understrappers," "menacing Russia with a perfumed cane"); and the comparison of Wellington to "the aquiline supremacy of the Cæsars" were worth preserving. But his John Russell is never right, and the letter to Brougham is an unsatisfactory shy at the widest target of the times. A more alarming section of this reliquary is filled with Disraeli's exercises in political light verse. These were ceremoniously conducted in the full Popian dignity of the heroic couplet. Wit at this period was attained by omitting the vowels. "From flippant F—nb—que down to priggish R——" is the sort of line that convulsed our fathers; and it cannot be denied that this method of openly concealed personalities gives the reader a pleasant sensation of being in the know. You feel that your neighbour is puzzling over R——, whilst you and young Mr. Disraeli and the right people are politely appreciating the exclusive jest. But the couplets are occasionally pointed, and

"Beneath his fostering care exchequers thrive,
  Bright sage, who proves that two and two make five,"

is almost a flash of prophecy. The other minor pieces
of the series are dialogues. Disraeli was not a master of the dialogue; there is a John Bull, who says
"Hem" and "Fiddle-faddle," and a self-conscious
conversation between Tomkins and Jenkins.

Of considerably greater interest is a series of articles in which the manner of Carlyle is deliberately
parodied: "Note ever, John, the difference between
a true nation-cry and a sham nation-cry. Reform
House of Commons, wise or unwise, true nation-cry;
Reform House of Lords, sham nation-cry." The
staccato Teutonism is not unskilfully caught;
and a later passage is really good parody: "Glory to
the Masses; choice, generous phrase! By no means
inert or cloddish; specially complimentary. What if
said Papineau orators and writers, by some mischance
of a *lapsus linguæ* or damnable error of the press, do
but omit the initial letter of that name, wherewith
they have defined, and in a manner baptized, their
countrymen?" Disraeli joins Swinburne and Mr.
Beerbohm in the excellent company of good paro-
dists.

An interesting feature of the whole collection is
the astonishing modernity of the views and phrases.

There is a family resemblance between Die-hards, whether their violent decease is to be a consequence of Reform or the Parliament Act; and the contours of last ditches are strikingly similar, whatever may be the measure when they obstruct. Disraeli is at his most ironical in denunciation of "the People"; like all representatives of a minority, he pours all his scorn on those who claim to speak for a majority; and like all reactionaries, he confines his constitutional affections to enactments of an engaging remoteness. In "The Vindication of the English Constitution," which is the most substantial piece that is preserved, Disraeli dedicated to Lord Lyndhurst a hundred pages of Tory constitutional theory. The rhapsodies, which are *fortissimo* about the Magna Carta, gradually diminish in volume until they reach the faintest acquiescence in the Whig Reform Act. The essay concludes with a lyrical demonstration that the Constitution of 1835 is a "complete democracy," which must have read strangely to the author of the Reform Act of 1867. The collection also enshrines the amazing statement that Louis Philippe resembled William III in his character. One might just as well scandalize Mr. Buckle by comparing Disraeli to Simon de Montfort.

MR. DELANE

YEARS ago, when a gentleman's collars impinged upon his cheeks and the Great Victorians were still in the nursery, the fivepenny *Times* was edited by John Thadeus Delane. Whilst ingenious persons were perfecting the Steam Locomotive and inventing the Electric Telegraph, its opinions were the admiration of his countrymen, its information was the envy of Cabinet Ministers, and its independence was the despair of foreign Sovereigns. It was, in fact, the High Old *Times*. Before the repeal of the newspaper stamp duty made possible what was elegantly termed "a Brummagem Press," young gentlemen in sealskin waistcoats scrutinized its sporting intelligence behind the ample paddle-boxes of the steam-packet, and old gentlemen in plaid rugs and travelling-caps read it anxiously in railway-trains to see whether Mr. Cobden had yet succeeded in ruining his unhappy country. Prince Albert called it a "wicked paper"; Lord Palmerston burnt it with the utmost regularity; and President Lincoln expressed the gratifying opinion that it had more power than anything in the world, with the possible exception of the Mississippi. In these pleasing circumstances the editor, in spite of an unimpressive academic career and that appearance which so many of his contemporaries shared with Mr. Matthew Arnold, was a person of importance.

It is one of the few consolations of statesmen that editors, who distribute immortality, themselves rarely attain it. The name of the Recording Angel is unknown to hagiologists; and his obscurity is commonly shared by his grosser competitors. Delane, who conducted *The Times* for thirty-six years, is almost the sole exception of his generation. He has earned an honourable interment in a full-length biography that any Premier might envy; and he is safe in his niche, with Lassalle and Admiral Maxse, in the novels of George Meredith. His reputation, unlike that of many editors, does not rest on the distinction of his contributors, although they included every eminent Victorian from Thackeray to Robert Lowe. But his fame is founded upon the solid achievement of *The Times* newspaper between the years 1841 and 1877. It is probable that his reputation originated in the exaggerated respect of his colleagues for his social career. A journalist who dined out and did not wear paper collars was something of a portent in the Sixties. But Delane emerges from the gradual publication of Victorian letters and diaries as something more than a journalist who was a gentleman. He was the ally and intimate of Lord Aberdeen when he was a pacifist, and of Lord Palmerston when (in his second and worse manner) he was a Jingo. He was the invariable counsellor of Lords Granville and Clarendon and a source of constant irritation to the Prince Consort. To the biographers of Bright, Gladstone, and Cobden he appears as a power of darkness, and Kinglake almost made him the villain of his dramatized version of the Crimea. Archbishop Tait was not far wrong when he observed that Delane's approaching resignation was almost as important an exit as the departure of Mr. Disraeli to the House of Lords.

One is enabled, in a rapid survey of thirty years of political history from the angle of Printing House Square, to hear the Minister suggest the policy to the editor (or frequently vice-versa), to read a sufficient extract from the full-mouthed eloquence in which it was announced by the leader-writer, and to see the comments of party leaders upon the value and effect of the departure. Sir Edward Cook was admirably qualified to write of Delane and his *Times;* he had a thorough knowledge of political history, journalism held no secrets for him, and his own experience in the mysterious *penetralia* of the Press

Bureau lent a peculiar poignancy to his treatment of the unbridled war-correspondence of W. H. Russell.

Delane had reached the respectable age of twenty-three when he was summoned by the reigning Walter to edit *The Times*. Queen Victoria had been four years on the throne, and everybody was engaged in building railways or buying railway shares; in the same year *Punch* was founded. His predecessor had succeeded by his fierce independence and interminable sentences in making the reputation of the paper; but it remained for Delane to elevate it to the rank of a public institution. His friendship with Lord Clarendon gave him a valuable access to the Foreign Office, and acquaintance with Charles Greville opened to *The Times* the flood-gates of his inexhaustible gossip. Four years later the startling publication of Sir Robert Peel's conversion to Free Trade marked his first triumph as a journalist and earned him his place in *Diana of the Crossways* as "Mr. Tonans . . . in his den at midnight."

Sir Edward Cook in an indignant footnote defends Mrs. Norton's reputation for discretion and manages to shift the guilt to Lord Aberdeen. It is improbable that he provided Delane with the definite statement which appeared in *The Times*, because that statement, when it was made, was not true. But, as

Lord Curzon has remarked, the business of journalists is the intelligent anticipation of future events; and Delane was a master of sensational deduction, as he showed when he founded an announcement that Lord Northbrook had been appointed Viceroy of India upon his reported enquiry whether a hot climate would suit a delicate girl.

His importance in politics rests upon his alliance with Lord Palmerston. In the earlier years, when that statesman was right, his international Radicalism was sternly opposed by *The Times*. But in the decade after the Crimea, when that statesman was indubitably wrong, his Conservatism at home and his truculence abroad earned Delane's loyal support; and the great editor was seen, to the admiration of his colleagues, at Lady Palmerston's evening parties. Like his leader, he talked nonsense about President Lincoln, and enquired whether his name was "ultimately to be classed in the catalogue of monsters, wholesale assassins and butchers of their kind"; but in the Crimea *The Times* invented war correspondents and saved the Army. Since the official courier was delayed by an accident and the Czar first saw the British ultimatum in his London paper, war was virtually declared against Russia by *The Times;* and that journal proceeded to conduct the campaign which it had thus opened. Delane exasperated Lord Raglan, encouraged Miss Nightingale, and is a candidate for the dubious distinction of having suggested the stroke against Sebastopol. It was a great achievement, that was hardly too well rewarded when Delane rode down Whitehall with a duke walking on each side of his horse.

M. ADOLPHE THIERS

It is perhaps something more than an affectation of Christmas to recognize in Adolphe Thiers and Camillo Cavour the Brothers Cheeryble of Latin statesmanship. There is an indefinable touch of Dickens about the way in which those two little men bob up into history. They button their tight little frock-coats, adjust their ill-fitting Victorian spectacles, and proceed with invincible benevolence to save their countries, whilst they beam upon their astonished countrymen. One is always expecting them to pay off a cruel mortgage, wipe away a tear, and leave the embarrassed hero with his blushing bride. Instead they made, to the profound disgust of the House of Hapsburg, the Kingdom of Italy, and saved, to the evident surprise of the House of Hohenzollern, the French Republic.

Of the two, Thiers probably deserved the most (as he has certainly obtained the least) reputation, by reason of the incredible range of his career. Cavour did his work in a single period between the disappointment of 1848 and the triumph of 1861. But the achievement of Thiers, which was the administration of France between 1871 and 1873, was the work of the ablest Minister of the last Government but two, and the leading historian of the last monarchy but three. He had as many careers as the Phœnix, and as many farewell performances as an actor-manager. In the year 1841 he was dismissed, like M. Delcassé in 1905, as the price of European peace; in the year 1851 he was demonstrably impossible in any combination, whether the Second Republic survived or the Second Empire came into existence; in the year 1861 he was an academic old gentleman who kept a *salon* and wrote history; but in the year 1871 he was President of the Republic and deputy for twenty-six constituencies, the embodiment of law and order, and the rising hope of the chancelleries of Europe. The Third Republic was nursed through its fractious and unfascinating infancy by a Minister of Louis-Philippe, and the little man, who had been a caller on Talleyrand, lived to share with M. Poincaré the anxious responsibility of controlling M. Clemenceau. It is an achievement unrivalled even by the dual career of Mr. Gladstone, who retired but once and was never confronted by so much as a single change of dynasty.

His *Notes et Souvenirs* from 1870 to 1873 form a vivid diary of his peace negotiations and Presidency.

The Grand Tour of the neutrals began in London, where he saw Lord Granville and Mr. Gladstone. He congratulates himself that *"The Times* itself has changed its tone for the better," a temporary phase which was probably due to the leading articles of Mr. Leonard Courtney. But Thiers did not know that Delane had rebuked this improper pacifism, and in any case British neutrality in the Franco-Prussian War was impenetrably passive. He had the intelligence to appreciate the German influence of the Court, although he was solemnly rebuked by Lord Granville as "a Minister of England" for having the indelicacy to mention it. Mr. Gladstone, who was unwilling to leave his axe at the foot of the Irish upas tree, was unmoved by the suggestion that England was missing in 1870 the opportunity which France had missed in 1866; and when Thiers emphasized this undignified abdication of any part in continental affairs, the Prime Minister "preserved a grieved and uncomfortable silence." From London the little man proceeded to Vienna, where the Saxon Chancellor gave him a more cordial reception. Austria had been buying cavalry horses; and it was hoped that the part of armed mediator would appeal to the South German renegade whom Bismarck had broken in 1866. But unfortunately Beust, who impressed Thiers with having, of all the men he had known, "the best air of believing what he says," was paralyzed by uncertainty as to the attitude of Russia. In order to resolve his doubts, the indomitable bagman of peace proceeded to St. Petersburg. The account of his Russian visit is perhaps the most important of his revelations, because it appears to antedate by five years the genesis of the Franco-Russian alliance. It is usual to trace the first movements in this direction during or just before the war scare of 1875. But there was apparently a conversation between Thiers and Gortchakoff in the autumn of 1870, in which the Chancellor replied to an offer of the French alliance:

We have always been promised this alliance, General Fleury spoke to us of it constantly, and we never saw it come to pass . . . however, to-day is not the moment to conclude it. Later we will take measures for uniting France with Russia; for the moment, let us consider the question of how to save her from the evil case in which she finds herself.

A few days later the Czar himself said:

I should most gladly obtain such an alliance with France, an alliance for peace, not for war and conquest.

It is a new chapter in the early history of the Dual Alliance.

From Russia Thiers proceeded to Italy and embarked at Florence on a singular negotiation which was to place 100,000 Italians in the neighbourhood of

Lyons, and compel the Germans by this pressure to abandon the siege of Paris. But the indefatigable, if elderly, dove was at length compelled to return to the Ark without either an olive-branch or an Italian army corps; and France was compelled to negotiate the terms of peace with Bismarck himself. In this transaction Thiers' principal efforts were directed to the preservation of the *territoire de Belfort*. It is entertaining in these days of soaring interest to remark his horror of borrowing at the "usurious rate of $7\frac{1}{2}$ per cent."; and the observation of Bismarck that neutral States "did not exist as far as he was concerned" is typical of a more ingenuous period of Prussian policy.

There are few things finer in European history than the exploit of this little Frenchman who set out at the age of seventy-three to find peace for his country in a tour of the neutral States. It is almost as though England were to be saved (although it is not easy to imagine from what) by Lord Halsbury. Thiers bargained with Bismarck for a treaty, swept the Commune out of Paris, hustled a royalist Assembly into a republican constitution, remade the French army, and paid off an indemnity which had shocked every financier in Europe. *Si monumentum quæris,* it is to be found in the Prussian war scare of 1875: France had been struck down in 1870, and the alarm of her enemies within five years is the best evidence of her recovery and the noblest tribute to the work of Thiers.　He was a little barrister and wrote history.

M. LÉON GAMBETTA

THE attitude of British opinion to foreign statesmanship was never better expressed than in a conversation *viva voce populi* overheard by Mr. Anstey some thirty years ago in the neighbourhood of the Marble Arch. An Irish patriot (patriotism was always an Irish export) was enlivening his hearers with a disquisition on the peculiar virtues of imprisonment (incarceration was ever an Irish pastime) as an inspiration and a stimulant:

. . . Some of the best and greatest men that ever lived have been in prison——

AN AUDITOR (*who seems to have reasons of his own for finding this argument particularly soothing*). 'Ear, 'ear!

THE IRISH PATRIOT. Look at Gambetta!

A DULL MAN (*to* NEIGHBOUR). *Wot's* he a-tellin' of us to look at?

HIS NEIGHBOUR. Gambetter.

THE DULL MAN. Gam— 'oo?

NEIGHBOUR (*curtly*). Better.

THE DULL MAN. Better nor *wot?*

It is in that mood of incredulity tempered with mild amusement that the bearers of foreign names are regarded in this country. It may be a legitimate revenge for the imbecility of those continental compositors who have systematically misprinted the name of every British minister since Pitt. But it affords a somewhat uncertain basis for the formation of historical estimates.

When one is confronted with the biography of a French minister by a French President, one feels proudly that this sort of thing could never have happened in England. The contributions of British statesmen to history are limited to their simple lives, their downright deeds, their collected speeches on political topics of immense, but happily ephemeral importance, and (in rare cases of immense culture) of their Inaugural Address to the British Bee-Keepers' Association on "Bees in Virgil." It is the peculiar distinction of our statesmanship that it is wholly illiterate. When one says of a common man that he had made his mark, one refers to his success in life; but when one says it of a British statesman, one may be taken to allude to the substitute for his signature. There have, of course, been exceptions, trifling, it is true, but none the less humiliating to those of us who care for the simple traditions of our public life. Lord Rosebery, whose name might otherwise have been honoured equally at Epsom and in Downing Street, has persistently held the pen with a skill that is positively professional; and Mr. Asquith never forfeited more Liberal confidence than on the day when he reprinted, with ineffable frivolity, an essay on De Quincey. It is an action which would be unthinkable in a Geddes. There are no novels by Dr. Macnamara; there is hardly so much as a short story by Mr. Bonar Law. The scanty leisure of Mr. Walter Long, the brief repose of Sir Edward Carson, the sorely interrupted rest of Mr. Shortt is not devoted to the questionable cultivation of the Muses, those alien young persons of certainly Greek, and probably Constantinist, extraction. Viscount Grey touched the utmost permissible limit of our concession to dilettantism, when he published a work on Fly-fishing; and the political career of Mr. Winston Churchill was seriously endangered by the popular belief that he was the real author of the works of his American namesake.

It is the British tradition that a politician may decline into literature in the same manner as he sinks into the Upper House. His Works must not be written until he is past work; and when he has lost his memory, he is at liberty to write his memoirs. That is why one arches an insular eyebrow at the information that M. Deschanel accepted, in the plenitude of his powers, an invitation to write the life of a deceased statesman. His country was in danger; he was actively engaged as President of the Chamber;

and there were at least six hundred men in English public life who could have informed him, under the provocation offered by his strange proceeding, that there was a war on. But he was undeterred by the oddity of his own action, and this remarkable foreigner put pen to paper in order that in those weeks of victory, when the marching columns of the French infantry swung down the long white roads into the little towns of Lorraine and Alsace, his countrymen might have once more the vision of that bearded, one-eyed man who flung an arm eastward in the years of defeat to point his haunting cry, *"Regardez la trouée des Vosges."* An Englishman who evoked such memories of the past would have been relegated to a professorship. M. Deschanel was elected President of the Republic.

Gambetta, like many Frenchmen of distinction, was not wholly free from French blood. His mother was the daughter of a country chemist in the *Midi,* and she married, a few weeks after the accession of Queen Victoria, an interesting foreigner who had come to Cahors from the Genoese Riviera in the grocery business. The bridegroom had once shipped as cabin-boy from an Italian port to Chili in a clipper, whose passenger list included a man who was to be General Garibaldi and a priest who was to be Pope Pius IX. But the experience made neither a mariner nor a *rasta* of him; and he settled amiably down to sell to the citizens of Cahors the unpleasing pottery of his native land. The prospect of a long life opened before his infant son when, at the age of four, he was given up by the doctors; and within forty years that half-Italian boy was the voice of France.

He graduated in the queer school from which the French draw their parliamentarians. After passing through a Lycée, in which his preceptors fed him upon the windy fruits of Athenian eloquence, he became in the last decade of the Second Empire a French national, a talker in cafés, and an ornament of the Parisian Bar. It was a strange profession, in which the art of voice-production was of considerably more importance than the science of jurisprudence; and a student in search of the best models could write home without incongruity, "*Je vais au théâtre et au Palais.*" The atmosphere was eminently congenial to a bull-necked young man from the *Midi,* and Gambetta attracted the favourable attention of his colleagues by a free use of imagery drawn from the Crucifixion in defence of a seditious workman. Success in this class of case went naturally hand in hand with the beginnings of a political career; and the one-eyed *avocat* with the black beard began to rank among the more conspicuous enemies of the Empire. His diapason was a not unwelcome addition to the chorus of hostility to Napoleon III, in which the peevish *vox humana* of Jules Favre vied with the shrill ululations of Mr. Swinburne and the deeper chest notes of Victor Hugo; until in 1868 a brief for a republican journalist brought him definitely into the centre of the stage.

A deputy named Baudin had got himself rather gratuitously shot during the *coup d'état* of 1851. For seventeen years his interrupted existence was ignored by his political sympathizers. But in the closing years of the Empire the researches of republican propagandists brought him to light as a promising excuse for the exercise of the French genius for political interments. It was unfortunately found impracticable to bury him: that had been done already. But there was yet time for a funeral oration or so; it was not too late for a trifle of monumental masonry. A subscription was opened for the visible commemoration of this somewhat dim figure of the republican mythology; and a brutal executive interrupted this agreeable pastime by prosecuting one of the journalists who opened the list. Gambetta (with him, a galaxy of republican talent) appeared for the defence. Having none, he indulged in the luxury of a counter-attack. It was developed along the whole front of Imperial policy; and by the engaging procedure of the French courts, in which relevance would appear to be the sole ground for excluding evidence, he was permitted to prosecute the prosecution. The Court was bullied, the Crown was shouted down, the gallery was electrified by an advocate who was Olynthiac, Verrine and Philippic by turns. At the fall of the curtain (surely one can hardly imagine a French trial terminated by anything less dramatic than a curtain) the applause was positively operatic; and within seven months the oracle of the Café Procope was deputy for Marseilles.

Gambetta had now achieved notoriety; and it was no longer necessary for him to conceal his intelligence. When the hot weather of 1870 sent Benedetti to Ems and the Second Empire to Sedan, it might have been expected from his past record that his contribution to the national effort would be confined to sonorous republicanism. But it was not. Like many men of mixed origin, he was intensely patriotic in the country of his adoption. In disagreement with seventeen of his political associates he voted the war credits of the Empire; and to the last he seemed more interested in the defeat of Prussia than in the eviction of the Bonapartes: it was, for a republican politician, the supreme sacrifice of an unrivalled opportunity. The Empire went down in the sunshine of September; and in its place a young Republic confronted the elderly ravishers of the Prussian General Staff. Militarily she was as unprepared before von Moltke and von Roon as Susanna, upon a similar occasion, before her elders. But the soul and centre of her military effort, heartening Paris, ballooning over the German lines, galvanizing the peripatetic Executive at Tours, was a man of thirty-two with one eye, whom an ambitious Italian parent had put to be a fine French lawyer; and his country rewarded him with twelve years of political importance, crowned by a dictatorship.

By a pleasing irony M. Deschanel set himself to write this tale of French defeat during the years of French victory; and his performance is as interesting for students of the subject as it is for that greater number who are students of the author. If it is within the power of the President of the Republic to initiate legislation, it would not be surprising if he tabled something drastic dealing with translations from the French. One can pardon a translator unfamiliar with the habits of French classicists who fails to recognize the Olynthiac Orations when they are disguised as *"Olynthiennes"*; and only an Orientalist would complain of the translation of *"l'échec de Lang-Son"* as "Lang-Son's fiasco," when the poor thing was the name of a defeat rather than that of a general. But it is hardly possible to forgive a travesty of M. Deschanel's emotional climax. The man lay dying, and a woman bent over him. *"Une femme le baisa au front et disparut dans l'ombre, à jamais."* M. De-

schanel has the genius for funeral oratory of all
French statesmen, but his translator is sadly puzzled
by the scene: "a woman," his victim is made to say
to the English reader, "a woman kissed him on the
forehead, and *he* vanished into the darkness for ever."
The italics, as they say, are ours; the sentiment is
not M. Deschanel's; and the theology is the translator's alone.

Gambetta was an ideal leader for a beaten country.
His proclamations did not win positions; and even the
advantage that she had lost her War Office was insufficient to bring France to victory. But by his
ill-shod *moblots* and his impromptu strategy he con-
trived through the short, black days of that snowy
winter of 1871 to exorcise the temper of defeat from a
defeated nation. Men have earned immortality for
less than that. It was the tragedy of the Peasants'
Revolt that it was a revolution which never found its
Danton, but only a handful of Héberts. It is the
bitterness of the German defeat that it has not yet
found its Gambetta.

GENERAL WALKER

It is always delightful, as Pygmalion discovered, to meet a piece of art that has come to life. An omnibus interior after Barry Pain or a War Cabinet by Gilbert and Sullivan is as attractive as the Rossetti goitre or the Beardsley lip. But there can be few encounters more charming than the discovery (in a most interesting work by a learned man who professes Economics and Sociology in the Louisiana State University) of a perfect Conrad. One has, as one meets him, a lazy sense of fireflies and a *chaise longue* in the tropics; there is an air of wise First Mates and Borneo cigars, and the comfortable feeling that we shall be told all about him by Captain Marlow, in thirty-six hours or so. It will be a story of sea-beaches in a hot climate, in which men of parts will muster incredible resources of gravity and introspection in order to do buccaneering things of the utmost simplicity. It will, in fact, have more than a little the air of a charade performance of *Treasure Island*, played by a cast of distinguished, but dissatisfied,

237

philosophers.   That is why I said that the career of Mr. Walker as a pirate was a perfect Conrad.

It is the peculiar distinction of William Walker that there stands in the chief square of the capital of Costa Rica, whose name escapes me, an elegant figure of a young lady trampling him in effigy.   To few men, unless indeed they chance to be the personal friends of sculptors (a limited class), does such an honour fall. It came to Walker because he followed, with the full energy of a man born in Nashville, Tennessee, the high calling of a filibuster.   He was the son of an insurance manager; and he became almost mechanically a pirate.   He graduated at the University of Nashville, where the curriculum included "algebra, geometry, trigonometry, descriptive and analytical geometry, conic sections, calculus, mensuration, surveying, navigation, mechanics, astronomy, chemistry, mineralogy, geology, experimental philosophy, natural history, Roman and Grecian antiquities, Greek and Latin classics, rhetoric and belles-lettres, history, mental and moral philosophy, logic, political economy, international and constitutional law, composition, criticism and oratory, natural theology, Christian evidences, and the Bible."   Any student of the works of Mr. Conrad will know that for a man of such accomplishments there was no opening elsewhere than under the black flag.

Walker's *floruit* as a filibuster was about the year
1850.   There is, at first sight, something faintly dis-
concerting in the occurrence of Filibuster Brown as
a national character at a time when most people
looked like daguerrotypes and sounded like Emerson.
His career against the regular background of American life in the Fifties has the effect of the tramp of
smugglers and a strong smell of French brandy in a
cellar under one of Miss Austen's parlours.   One
seems to be sitting on the horsehair of an early drawing-room by Mr. Henry James, whilst odd men in
ear-rings insist on counting doubloons (or is it pis-
toles?) in the next room.   That is the charm, although
it was not felt by his contemporaries, of William
Walker.   His beginnings were as docile as his contemporary background.   Having graduated in the
numerous accomplishments of the University of
Nashville, he studied medicine and became an M.D.
of the University of Pennsylvania. Then, embodying
in himself the combined educational ideals of Mr. H.
G. Wells and Mr. A. C. Benson, he moved on to the
easy slope that led to piracy and was admitted to the
Bar in New Orleans.   Now the law of Louisiana is
known to be founded principally upon the *Code
Napoléon*; and the sinister career of William Walker
neatly illustrates the disastrous influence of codifica-
tion on the character of one who, under a happier

system of jurisprudence, might have become one of our most respected jurists.

The rake's progress through the professions continued; and in the year 1848, when the European market for revolutionaries was rising sharply, Walker sank a stage lower and began to write for the Press. He even edited a paper called *The Crescent*, which so far diverged from the ideals of its title as to wane rather than to wax; and he prosecuted a remarkable love affair with a young lady who was congenitally deaf. It has been frequently observed that love is blind; but its deprivation of the other senses is a less usual phenomenon. The idyll of William Walker should be told with the stern pathos of Dr. Scroggs's narrative:

To his many other accomplishments Walker now added the sign language of deaf mutes and proceeded to press his suit. One story has it that his love was not returned; another, that his affection was reciprocated, but that a misunderstanding caused an estrangement; and still another, that they were happy in their love and had actually fixed the date for the wedding. It matters little which of these statements is true, for the outcome, so far as Walker was concerned, was the same. The city was scourged by one of its visitations of yellow fever, and Helen Martin was an early victim.

That is the supreme, the Conrad touch.

One is now at the brink of the period in which

Walker filiburst (if that is the appropriate aorist). After an uneventful residence in San Francisco, in which he failed to induce the authorities to do anything more stimulating than imprison him for contempt of court, he bought an astonishing suit of clothes and crossed the Mexican frontier. An American traveller who met him at Guaymas brought back an indelible impression of his appearance:

> His head was surmounted by a huge white fur hat, whose long knap waved with the breeze, which, together with a very ill-made, short-waisted blue coat, with gilt buttons, and a pair of grey, shapeless pantaloons, made up the ensemble of as unprepossessing-looking a person as one would meet in a day's walk.

Having acquired the pirate's make-up, Walker cast round for the remainder of the outfit. He returned to San Francisco and placed on the market a number of bonds of the Republic of Sonora, which did not exist. He further loaded a brig with ammunition and camp equipment; and when the authorities seized it, he recovered the vessel in replevin and sued the military for trespass. It is not for nothing that members of the Bar take to piracy. Then, with the impressive rank of Colonel of the Independence Regiment, he sailed for Sonora. As a beginning, he captured the Governor of La Paz and created in a three-line proclamation the Republic of Lower California, which was at once endowed by this far-sighted practitioner with the only system of jurisprudence with which he was personally familiar, the Civil Code and the Code of Practice of the State of Louisiana. Narrow critics have believed that his motive was a desire to import the Louisianian institution of slavery. But it must be obvious that his ruling anxiety was strictly professional; he was determined that, on his elevation to the South Californian bench, he should be decently familiar with the law which he would have to administer. For the moment, however, he preferred the executive to the judicature; and he became President of the new republic, whilst the *opéra bouffe* capture of another Mexican Governor was effected, and American sympathizers opened a recruiting-office at the corner of Sacramento Street, San Francisco. The pleasant climate favouring the growth of tropical republics, he proceeded shortly to fulminate, in a further body of proclamations, the Republic of Sonora. Then his supporters failed him; and, after a gentle cavalry action with a Mexican patrol, he surrendered to the United States authorities on an undertaking to stand trial in San Francisco for violating the neutrality laws. Filibustering now seems to have entered on a period of litigation that must have warmed Walker's professional heart. Captains, majors, surgeons, Mexican consuls, and even Walker's Secretary of State passed through the dock in rapid succession. Meanwhile the ports of the Pacific Slope pullulated with war material, and the oddest people sailed for Mexico to interrupt the eternal repose of the Latin races with the methodical genius for efficiency and self-government of the Anglo-Saxon.

Each of Walker's ventures was conducted on the model of his first effort. An invitation to Nicaragua was followed by an expedition to Granada. Here Walker's old professional habits reasserted themselves; this time, instead of importing his own Code, he started a newspaper. There was a succession of executions and a war with Costa Rica. Then, in a confused way, Wall Street came in. The reigning Vanderbilt, who was hostile to the filibuster republic, got control of a shipping company and tried to cut Walker's communications with the United States; and the course of events became almost invisible behind that whirl of litigation and "bear raids" which is the native air of the American financier. Walker, who had now become President of Nicaragua, endeavoured to accredit a Minister to the Court of St. James's; he was an old gentleman with a long grey beard, which he had vowed never to shave until the Spanish evacuated Cuba. But in spite of this tonsorial distinction His Excellency never presented his credentials in Downing Street. Walker was next threatened by a *triplice* of Guatemala, Honduras, and San Salvador, which rang down the Wilhelm-strasse and echoed across the Ballplatz and resounded along the Quai d'Orsay. If universal unpopularity was the test of universal empire, his Napoleonic isolation qualified Walker for a pedestal inscribed *Gulielmus Perambulator, Imperator Omnium Americarum.* Costa Rica (how one remembers the reverberation of it in the Chancelleries of the world) came in; and the filibuster experiment closed after an exciting campaign over ground which is principally familiar to philatelists. A second venture in Nicaragua and a descent on Honduras terminated his activity. Like the other Man of Destiny, he surrendered to the captain of a British warship. But the *Icarus* (it may have been due to some flaw in the mythology) was less hospitable than the *Bellerophon;* and Walker was handed over to the ungrateful people of Honduras. They shot him without hesitation in the angle of a wall outside Truxillo; and a gentleman on *Harper's Weekly* compared the United States Government's discouragement of his operations to the attitude of the Church of England towards Knox, Whitefield and Wesley. You will have noticed the resemblance.

SUPERMEN

II.   PRIMITIVES

King Alfred
King John
King Hal
Lady Hamilton
Herr V. Treitschke
Mr. Wilfrid Blunt
P. T. Barnum

KING ALFRED

THE trouble about King Alfred has always been one's complete inability to distinguish him from King Arthur and Prince Albert. It may be because Count Gleichen once made a statue of him; or because he was (to say the least of it) a good man. But anyway the discreditable fact remains that I have never been quite sure whether he married Guinevere or Queen Victoria. It is a confusion that historians have done little to correct; because the need of a paragon in early history, which drove the Roman poets to the doctrine of the Golden Age, has been satisfied in the case of Alfred by the creation of a mythical monarch with many of the gifts of Napoleon and most of the qualities of Abraham Lincoln. The unfortunate king has become oppressed with the intolerable burden of his virtues; and he is by this time so many-sided as to be almost completely invisible from any point of view. It has resulted that a bewildered posterity, finding itself debarred from any appreciation of a most interesting military and political career during the Danish invasion of England, has clung convulsively to the glorious circumstance that King Alfred defied the proverb by burning his cake at both ends and eating it too. It is an inadequate record of a busy life.

If Alfred had been a Frenchman, he would have had at least three standard and classical biographies; and if he had been a German, the All-Highest House would have founded a university for the exclusive study of Its illustrious ancestor. As it is, the English bibliography of the first great King of England is almost as large as that of a minor Napoleonic Marshal. Anglo-Saxon reticence may sometimes be carried too far. But it is ungracious to complain that the business of writing a definitive text-book upon Alfred has been so long delayed, when the result is so completely satisfactory. His latest biographer follows the texts closely; but she is not so acutely afflicted with the Anglo-Saxon attitude as most Oxford historians, who tend to degenerate on the slightest provocation into Freemanesque maunderings about *Eorlings* and *Ceorlings*. It is true that in a moment of weakness she refers to the King as *Engelondes deorling,* a phrase immortalized, with slightly better spelling, by the late Poet Laureate. But apart from an occasional lapse into the ridiculous vernacular of her ancestors, she has put the story of Alfred into a clear, scholarly and accurate volume. The only inadequate thing in the book is a map, which serves to reduce the reader to a state of geographical ignorance almost equal to that of the great Saxon strategist himself.

The true history of Alfred, Ethelwulf's son, is the record of a painstaking, Teutonic fighting man, who was incidentally the father of his country. Alfred was not an inspired soldier; but he possessed the supreme military virtue of willingness to be taught by the enemy. He was hardly the founder of the British navy; although he has become the eponymous saint of the Blue Water School on the strength of a number of vessels of peculiar design, and a fortunate gale which arrived before the king had completed his building programme, and sent, according to the Chronicle, one hundred and forty enemy ships "to the devils." And, above all, he was not the indifferent pastry-cook of popular myth or the queer mystical figure of the interpolations to Asser, with his mysterious prayers and diseases and a general flavour of the late Middle Ages or the early Nineties. But he was just a careful man of moderate ability, with a strong interest in the welfare of his subjects and a mild taste for science and literature. King Alfred was really rather like Prince Albert after all.

Of his youth and education there is little to say. Some may regret that history does not permit him to display the indecent precocity of the copybook, but rather the juvenile imbecility of true greatness. But the deficiencies of his early training enabled him to display in later years a quiet determination to acquire the learning that he had missed in boyhood, which almost equals Cato's intellectual heroism when he learned Greek greybearded. His importance to England begins in the year 868 with his appointment as *Secundarius* to his brother the king. Three years later in the *Année Terrible* of the Saxon kingdom Alfred's trial opened. Reading was seized by the Danes; and the failure of a Saxon attack upon their entrenchments illustrated the value of prepared positions and taught Alfred the first of his lessons in Danish methods of warfare. That singular people was in the habit of approaching a country in its ships, digging itself in, and making great cavalry raids on stolen horses from the shelter of its entrenched camp. It would appear that the Vikings were the original Horse Marines. The lessons of the Danish wars, like those of the American Civil War, were "spades and mounted infantry." Alfred learned them, and retired to Athelney to organize the national resistance.

When he emerged from his retreat, "and his people was fain of him," he swept the Northmen back into the north-east in the campaign of Ethandun. As the king moved out of Athelney on Brixton Deverill, the levies of Somerset, Wiltshire, and part of Hampshire moved up like the concentrating units of a modern army. On the very next day he moved his forces with Prussian rapidity upon Leigh, and then to the battlefield of Ethandun. The Danes collapsed before his complete and punctual concentration. This was something more than a laborious imitation of Danish nobility, it was a brilliant employment of punctuality and organization, factors that had been forgotten in European warfare since the hollow square of the Roman Empire went down before the Dervish rush of the Barbarians.

Alfred employed his years of peace in careful organization. The army was organized in two relays, like Nehemiah's wall-builders; the creation of Burhs applied a system of barbed wire and blockhouses to the restriction of the movements of a mobile enemy; and an increase in the number of Thanes substituted a professional soldiery for the heroic but incompetent amateurs of the earlier Saxon wars. After a second interval of war, Alfred proceeded with the organization of peace; Wessex was systematically divided into shires, and a collection of laws embodied all that was respectable in the earlier codes. The king himself exhibited an intense interest in the science of geography and a straightforward desire to supply his country by education with "men of prayer, men of war, and men of work." His literary career, for which his biographers appear to feel a somewhat exaggerated respect, consists for the most part of a blameless course of translations of improving works. Alfred had lived with a purpose, and fought with a purpose; and it was perhaps inevitable that he should write with a purpose.

KING JOHN

SEVEN hundred years ago, on a hot morning in the Thames valley, King John set seal to a Latin document of sixty clauses. It is a scene which has impressed imaginations as far apart as the Earl of Halsbury and the late Madame Tussaud; and the occasion possesses an interest beyond the theatrical value inherent in any meeting of persons in full armour so near to Waterloo Station. The banality of most anniversaries finds appropriate expression in the vulgarity of most monuments. But Magna Carta is perhaps entitled to more respectful treatment. The document itself, although it has been belittled by the sinister combination of a Frenchman, a Scotchman, and a learned lady, is at least as important as any other that is honoured with an anniversary. If President Wilson was entitled to indicate by fireworks his satisfaction at the exclusion from the Eastern States of the authority of George III, there seems no reason why the Church of England should not celebrate by bonfires, if it feels inclined, its liberty to elect Bishops without the interference of King John.

The anniversary of Magna Carta shares with all other events before the Eighteenth Century the peculiar charm that we celebrate it, by reason of a change in the calendar, on the wrong day. In any case it should be remembered that we are not asked to make it an annual celebration, but only a centenary. And centenaries come but once a century.

Perhaps the foremost interest of the anniversary does not lie in the event itself, but in the chain of centenary years which lie between any modern June and the June when the Great Charter was signed. In 1315 no one had heard of it; and in 1415 men were more interested in the precarious situation of an Expeditionary Force in France, commanded by Henry V, which four months later cut its way through to the victory of Agincourt. In 1515 supercilious devotees of the New Learning regarded King John's barons as savages; but in 1615 those London lawyers, who were later to make the English Revolution, respected in an age of absolute monarchy the charter of personal liberty. In 1715 England was still debating the question whether the Treaties of Utrecht were an honourable peace and wishing that King George I would learn just a little English; and in 1815 King John was eclipsed by the news that the

English army was in Flanders and Napoleon was on the Sambre.

There is perhaps a malicious appropriateness that in 1915, when the centenary of Waterloo could only be celebrated on the spot by the Prussians, the anniversary of Magna Carta should have come round under the genial provisions of the Defence of the Realm Act. If any of our Major-Generals had heard of Stephen Langton, there can be little doubt that Runnymede would have been a prohibited area.

The proceedings of that June day, in "the meadow which is called Runingmede between Windelesore and Stanes," were in themselves a profoundly unimportant negotiation which appeared to terminate a singularly unimpressive rebellion. The noblemen of England had expressed their objection to compulsory military service in the French war by appearing in arms against the King. He was an unpleasant man and a good sportsman, who died four years later of an inability to assimilate peaches and new cider in the atmosphere of Newark. He had shown a certain resource in condemning an archdeacon to death by the pressure of an enormous leaden mitre; and his receipt of the news of the death of his First Minister with the observation, "Tell him to go to hell," exhibited a gift of limited but powerful repartee. On the present occasion he had travelled from Wiltshire by way of Oxford to interview the "Army of God and Holy Church." Since he noticed that it considerably out-numbered his own forces, he signed Magna Carta.

By reason either of the unique circumstance that the party of reform was led by the Archbishop of Canterbury, or of the simple fact that English poli-ticians are unfamiliar with the Latin language, the edict of King John has become the charter of English liberties. It is a splendid legacy, which would sur-prise no one more than the testator. English jurists have chosen to see in the thirty-ninth article of Magna Carta the right of all Englishmen to trial by twelve of their countrymen:

"Nullus liber homo capiatur vel imprisonetur . . . nisi per legale judicium parium suorum vel per legem terrae."

The Latin is sufficiently British to enshrine the Anglo-Saxon right of trial by jury; but whether King John contemplated this wide interpretation is a ques-tion that only his late majesty can answer. His sur-prise at his elevation to the ranks of the Fathers of the Constitution must be almost greater than that of his new neighbours. That, at any rate, is the clause which the King accepted at the suggestion of two Archbishops, seven Bishops, a Papal Legate, and sixteen Barons; and it is upon that democratic barri-cade that Lords Halsbury and Parmoor were prepared to fall in the cause of personal liberty and the name of Stephen Langton.

By the consent of eighteen generations of Englishmen, Magna Carta is one of the central documents of English history. But whereas the Grand Remonstrance was drafted by men who intended to remonstrate, and the Bill of Rights was a conscious attempt to pass the right into law, the chief contribution of Magna Carta to English law was the unintentional aberration of an absent-minded king. Magna Carta was an unpremeditated achievement, comparable to Simon de Montfort's, who looked once for a party-meeting and discovered the Parliament of the Three Estates, or to the somnambulist statesmanship of those men of the Eighteenth Century, who went out in search of an export trade and found an Empire.

KING HAL

THEY say that in the Fifteenth Century the Middle
Age went mad and shocked itself before it died. The
grey austerity of the Gothic, in which six generations
of men had glorified God by the chill, slim magnificence of their tall cathedrals, writhed into the rococo
convolutions of the Flamboyant manner, until it blos-
somed into that strange flower of mediæval decadence,
the Sainte Chapelle. Manners took on that air of conscious archaism which always marks the end of an
age. Priests became more priestly, maidens faltered
more maidenly, and knights bore themselves more
knightly than they had ever been seen in the real
world of priests, knights and maidens; and the whole
generation clung to the ways of its fathers with the
desperation of men who see clearly that their sons
will take a different road. It is not surprising that
there was born into this world of deliberate mediæval-
ism and self-conscious chivalry a king whose whole
career typified to the point of travesty the royal life
of the Middle Ages. Henry V, in whom a hasty pos-

terity has been sometimes overapt to see a handy summary of the mediæval monarchs, was in reality an ingenious reconstruction of his predecessors in the heroic age. But then posterity, poor dear, is so American: she *loves* epitomes, and the temptation to take Henry II, Edward III, Philip Augustus and several Dukes of Burgundy all in one by getting up King Henry V has proved too strong for her. He is, to say truth, a somewhat dubious antique. One feels all the time that he has been subjected to a drastic process of restoration. The colours have been heightened and the wormholes have been deepened. His chivalry was so much more chivalrous, his Round Table so infinitely rounder, and his castles so far more castellated than the real thing, that one may walk admiringly round him as though he were a mediæval masterpiece of that art of architectural reconstruction with which the ingenious M. Viollet-le-Duc delighted the contemporaries of Napoleon III.

This king, if one may adopt the language of the sale-room, was Sheraton at best; and his misfortune is that he is generally sold as Chippendale. But his career, if one is free from these antiquarian scruples, forms an excellent subject for biography. After all, he lived a long time ago. 1415 was not the day before yesterday, even if it was not at the heart of the Middle Ages. Knights were very sufficiently bold then, in spite of the disturbing element introduced into the gentlemanly pastime of war by the grimy innovation of artillery; and one may make his career the foundation of an interesting piece of mediæval history. One begins with a fine confused picture of England when Henry IV was engaged in making it, and his aristocracy was (like Penelope) unmaking it when his back was turned. One passes to the Shakesperean controversy as to the reality or otherwise of Prince Henry's wild oats: this is where one gets one's possibilities of comic relief, whilst mild-eyed historians titter like maiden aunts over the naughtiness of princes. When one gets Henry on the throne, the narrative takes on a broader sweep and becomes co-extensive with the course of Anglo-French history between 1413 and 1422.

Prince Hal (one falls inevitably into the dialect) had a birthplace, which was one of those periodical concessions which the British monarchy makes to Welsh susceptibilities. He was born at Monmouth on the Welsh border, in one of the fortresses which had been erected by English civilization to dam back the eastward-setting tide of Celtic barbarism; and it does infinite credit to the rapacity of Welsh tradition that he has been greeted, in these circumstances, as a Welsh hero. Early, perhaps too early, he went to Oxford; since the age of eleven seems unduly tender for an undergraduate, even after one has made allowance for the morbid precocity invariably displayed by heirs to the British throne. But as his residence was limited to a period of six months, the Oxford influence on his formation was of the slightest; and time was even wanting for the resident preceptors to proclaim those indications of exceptional ability, which they have never failed to detect in the sons of the very great. The remainder of his education (it was conducted in a Bishop's house, and the school-bills included eightpennyworth of harp-strings, a fourpenny work on grammar, and a new scabbard) would appear to have been confined to instruction in the local colour of the Middle Ages.

His real training began when his father sent him to govern the Crown Colony of Wales. Owen Glendower, who was (like most national heroes, from Pym to Robespierre) a lawyer, had raised the country behind the English garrison. He possessed the rare accomplishment of causing snow in August, and his Welsh *guerilleros* enjoyed the more substantial assistance of the French, who operated from the coast, and exhibited in the interest of the Welsh that burning sympathy with small nationalities which is always experienced by the enemies of large nations. This war, and the succeeding period of feudal confusion which resulted in the elimination of the Percies from the governing class, provided Prince Henry with his education in military statesmanship; and when he inherited the throne, he took with avidity to that recognized form of sport, a war with the French, which provided the Kings of England with an appropriate and dignified pastime before the public-spirited institution of Newmarket Heath by King Charles II as a substitute.

If his biographers have a fault, it is that they are a trifle inclined, as military historians, to exaggerate the intelligence of mediæval warfare. Strategy in the Middle Ages was an affair of mere collision. If a malicious fate brought the vaguely roaming armies in contact, there was a battle, and the ingenuity of generations of historians would be exercised in attributing to the respective commanders a depth and a precision of military design of which they were profoundly innocent. If, however, the collision was averted by some stroke of luck or loot, there was no battle, and the campaign is reduced in the text-books to the rank of a mere raid. The exercise of writing military history upon these terms is an entertaining one; and as it has brought merited fame, ennoblement, and a seat in the House of Commons to Sir Charles Oman, we must not deny to young historians this opportunity to place their foot upon the first rung of the professional ladder.

KING HAL

With the historical problem presented by Prince Henry as *viveur* his biographers are even more satisfactory than when they attempt an apology for his persecution of the Lollards. One finds it somehow difficult to see this cross between Haroun-al-Raschid and St. Louis presiding at the burning of the heretic Badby; and the fact that the prince interrupted the *auto-da-fé* in order to offer to a half-charred man a pension of one and ninepence a week for the sale of his soul cannot leave as favourable an impression on all minds as it has on that of an Oxford historian. But the soul of Oxford is sometimes above souls.

LADY HAMILTON

THE trouble with Lady Hamilton is that Nelson left her to the nation, when he ought to have left her to Sir William Hamilton. Perhaps it was because the nation is the normal legatee of pictures; and Emma was in herself the collected works of Romney. At any rate, this singular legacy of a beautiful woman and her daughter was not appreciated by its inheritors. It is an old quarrel whether her unhappiness was the work of an ungrateful nation; and there is small need to argue it now. It is quite possible that an unobtrusive and adequate pension might have been found for Lady Hamilton after Trafalgar. But she was not content to live inconspicuously upon the Consolidated Fund; all the best people did it, but Emma was a *parvenu*. She thirsted for recognition, like any trade union; and, having learnt heroics in the kitchen, she saw the dramatic value of her position as Nelson's quasi-widow and was indisposed to sit like Patience on the Nelson Monument. The results were seen in her ten years' tragedy between Trafalgar and Waterloo.

They were not years of neglect, unless notoriety is neglect; and they need not have been years of poverty, if she had learnt how to keep a fortune. But it was from this period, when she was blackmailed by Sicilians, persecuted by conveyancers, and imprisoned in the King's Bench, that her career got its peculiar flavour of futility. She had a past; but she had no future, which (as any grammarian can see) is highly irregular, and forms a striking contrast to that greater Emma who was the inspiration of Wilkins Micawber. The decline and fall of her empire is the chief cause of its fame. If Lady Hamilton had disappeared in 1805, she would have figured as largely in English history as Walewska or Georges in the history of the First Empire. But "Emma forlorn and weeping for Nelson" is a person to write about; and the biographers have buzzed round her memory like the duns round her front door.

Her beginnings are interesting to the collector; but one feels that most of her biographers might have given us a little more life with Nelson and a little less life below stairs. Emma Lyon was the child of an affair at Hawarden, although her meteoric career was more suggestive of Hughenden; and we may, if we feel that she should be ushered into the world with a blast on the trumpet of the *Family Herald,* accept the story which gives her a gentleman for a father.

He became an amateur blacksmith, and died of a consumption that may be described with a more than Five Towns' gusto. Like all literary babies, little Emma "crowed" in the pages of her biographies; she also became astonishingly pretty, and went into service as a nursemaid. Somewhat injudiciously she was removed to a situation in London, and was promoted kitchen-maid. She lost the place on account of some amateur theatricals, conducted in her mistress's clothes on the kitchen table; and with a stage-struck colleague she applied to Sheridan for a part at Drury Lane. She was rejected, and was assisted to a less desirable situation by a man called Angelo. It may be the misfortune of the subject rather than the fault of her biographers, but from this point all the old men are unpleasant old men, and none of the young men are nice young men.

A sea-captain, a baronet, and Charles Greville pass rapidly across the stage, until, by a singular transaction, she was transferred by Charles to his uncle, Sir William Hamilton, who married her and made her Ambassadress of His Britannic Majesty at Naples. In Naples, which was ruled by a stupid king who kept a cookshop, she formed a valuable friendship with the Queen. Emma was a singular acquaintance for the daughter of Marie Theresa; but royalty could not be too particular in the year 1793. She learned to spell late in life; but even as Ambassadress she wrote "the King and me sang duetts 3 hours." In Naples Emma met Nelson, who was in charge of the Mediterranean blockade; and there, rather than in England, she lived out the best years of her life. So in Naples one may bid her, in her own orthography, "Adue."

HERR V. TREITSCHKE

THERE is a story of Canon Hannay's about a lady who broke out in the same week as the war; but she was nothing to the literary gentlemen. In those first days of August, when the war swept across Europe like the wind out of Africa, there was an ugly rush of innumerable Pilots to weather the Storm. Mr. Wells hurried into his oilskins; Mr. Arnold Bennett jumped into his sea-boots; and the Poet Laureate heaved a melodious but archaic lead. By the fifth day of the French mobilization the autumn publishing season was in full swing; and the Society of Authors clustered round Sir Edward Grey, ingeminating, like Wilkins' Emma, that it would never desert him. It was as though the usual old gentleman in the usual *Punch* cartoon had enquired from his window, "Watchman, what of the night?" and had been answered by the clear utterance of eight novelists, five poets, and Mr. Joseph McCabe. The mast was almost invisible under the mass of colours that had been nailed to it, and Mr. Kipling alone kept silence at the coming in of war: it was the silence of a realist confronted with reality.

Quite apart from its agreeable literary consequences (Mr. William Archer wrote an epic poem), this outburst produced a startling effect upon the war itself. The distinguished literary men who made it, were determined to save the State. The only difficulty was to find, at short notice, some one to save it from. We had for a few days the inspiring spectacle of a crowd of Ciceros looking for Catilines round every corner; and since one can hardly save one's country from people that one does not know, they very properly decided to save it from some one of whom they had already heard. Being unfamiliar with the Germans of the General Staff, our guardian authors resolved unanimously to save us from the Germans of the study. Moltke was a name to them and Schlieffen was even less; but they had all read Nietzsche in the Nineties, and Treitschke was a familiar type of the Continental Anglophobe. That is how the war of armies became suddenly, and to its intense surprise, a war of ideas: it was a startling triumph of the penetrating pen over the unintelligent sword. Great Britain had executed a perfectly normal and proper intervention in favour of the balance of European power and against the possibility of a hostile control of the Low Countries. It was a *casus belli* that Bolingbroke could have understood and Canning would have applauded. But the authors of England discovered in it a forlorn hope led by the British diplomatic service against the perverted philosophy of Central Europe. That is how the Dual Alliance of Nietzsche and Treitschke was called into existence to hang like twin Boneys over the happy homes of England. It is a strange *galère* for a respectable war. The War of the Spanish Succession, which was fought for a very similar object, had a very similar opening. Louis XIV aspired to the control of Western Europe, and, as is usual on these occasions, violated Belgian neutrality. Great Britain very properly, though somewhat reluctantly, intervened; but nobody announced to the startled subjects of William III that they were engaged in a *jehad* against the immoral philosophy of Pascal and Bossuet, as illustrated by the French king's violation of the Barrier Treaty.

The truth is that wars, since they have ceased to be legitimate forms of religious controversy, are not wars of ideas; and in the present instance the selection of two writers as villains of the piece was unusually inept. The choice was not happy, because their names (unlike "Huns" and "guns") would not rhyme in any circumstances—even when set to music; and the connection of one of them with any operations of

German policy had been singularly slender. Nietzsche, whose name has struck terror into a thousand sewing parties, was a remote and philosophic Pole. His contribution to the plot appears to be that, in the intervals of "a certain liveliness" with Wagner, he believed in force. But so did Carlyle; and no one has yet demanded the destruction of Chelsea or suggested that the *Landsturm* went on its wicked, Carlylean way from Ghent to Warsaw to the Lowland lilt of "It's a long, long way to Ecclefechan."

The second villain was more obviously entitled to a place in the cast. The trouble with Treitschke is that he was a German. At a time when all respectable persons east of the Rhine were Saxons or Bavarians, or Mecklenburgers, Treitschke was a truculent, anti-particularist German. It all came of reading history, which has undermined so many bright intelligences. Of course, he was not a German by extraction; but nationalists are rarely autochthonous. Patriots are made and not born; and there is nothing in Treitschke's blend of Bohemian ancestry with Prussian patriotism to startle a generation which is familiar with the Imperialism of Napoleon, who was not a Frenchman, or of Disraeli, who was not an Englishman. Treitschke's family were Czechs called Trschky; but they were persuaded, upon their immigration into Saxony, to substitute for that engaging sternutation a name that was less strikingly consonantal. Treitschke, however, although he retained in his ideas and in his controversial method some trace of the militant Protestantism which had centred in the Tyn Church of Prague, was born north of the Riesengebirge, and his father had been a soldier of some distinction in the Saxon army. It was only twenty years since Prussia had failed narrowly to obtain European sanction for the annexation of Saxony; and in a Saxon household Prussia was hated more bitterly than the French. This education produced in Treitschke an inevitable reaction. The air was full of a vague nationalism; and the universities, when he went there, were the preserve of the *vieilles barbes* of 1848. After Olmütz, where Prussia suffered humiliation at the hands of Austria, the Hohenzollerns were regarded almost as the martyrs of the German cause; and when Treitschke went to Freiburg as a graduate of half the universities in South Germany, he worshipped Prussia with the full enthusiasm of a man who lived in Baden.

At Freiburg he developed still further his fierce detestation of *Kleinstaaterei*. The small States of Germany were not an inspiring spectacle; and Treitschke found himself in sympathy with Bismarck's elimination of the Middle States and Offenbach's later ridicule of the *Grande-Duchesse de*

Gerolstein. An educated man revolted inevitably
against the unintelligence of Rhenish Clericals, who
looked alternately to Vienna and to Rome, and
against the unimportance of minor royalty, which
looked exclusively at itself. Treitschke with his
Prussian sympathies could not acquiesce in the media-
tized motto "Beust will be Beust"; and he discerned
in the Hohenzollern a dynasty that had done something for itself and for Germany, and in their present
Minister a man who might do more. In the year of
Sadowa Bismarck summoned him to Berlin and
offered him a place in the Prussian Press Bureau; it
was refused, and Treitschke departed to a chair at
Kiel. There he endeavoured without marked success
to impress upon the undergraduates of Schleswig-
Holstein their place in German history; and he returned with obvious relief to Heidelberg. From
this point Treitschke's academic career became an
easy course of official preferment. In 1864 he had
urged Prussia to annex the Danish Duchies:

The good cause will triumph, the heirs of Frederick the
Great will reign in Schleswig-Holstein, and in a short time
the nation will be ashamed of its own stupidity.

In 1870 he argued the case for the annexation of
Alsace-Lorraine on the sound military basis that "we
only demand the German lands of France and so

much Romance land as is necessary for their security." His admission of military necessity as a test for the traces of frontiers has been as fatal to a defeated Germany as his later admission, made in the hopes that Germany would one day be an African or Asiatic Power, that coloured troops may be used in European warfare, was unpalatable to a Germany at war with Algerian France and Indian England.

As a lecturer and historian Treitschke developed two things which have made him a name to most of us. In company with most continental observers, he believed that England was in a state of hopeless decay, and that the colonies, which it had obtained by fraud, might be removed by force, differing from Victor Hugo only in the view that Germany rather than France was the expectant heir. He was driven to this conclusion by a profoundly interesting philosophy of English history, which was not much further from the truth than most English readings of Continental history. His indignation was very properly stirred by the spectacle of the weak "John Bull" allied with the palsied Turk; and he offered the disinterested suggestion of an Anglo-Russian alliance. The suggestion has been gratefully acted on. But the neo-Turkish cry of *Deutschland über Allah* is hardly consistent with Treitschke's pronounced preference for the destruction of Turkey.

HERR V. TREITSCHKE

His second and more notorious contribution to politics is the theory of international contract, that

all treaties under international law embody the clause *rebus sic stantibus.* The State has no higher Judge above it, and will therefore conclude all treaties with that mental reservation.

It is extremely bad law; but it is exceedingly good Prussian history.

The strangest thing about Treitschke's career is that it was purely academic. He definitely became one of the wild-eyed prophetic lecturers of the Sixties, who paced the rostrum like a quarterdeck. There appears to be a place in German politics for the academic person, a fact which enabled Treitschke, who was completely deaf, to gain a hearing from the Reichstag, which he could not hear. The academic person has been less fortunate in his intrusions into the politics of other countries. Sir Richard Jebb sat for years at Westminster without importing into the proceedings of the House of Commons much of the level mood of Sophocles; Mr. Herbert Fisher (it is profoundly to his credit) has never really gone into politics; and of Dr. Wilson, who deserted a Chair for a throne and left the throne for one of those eminences from which one is privileged to view all the kingdoms of the earth in highly undesirable company, it is too early, perhaps it will always be too early, to speak.

MR. WILFRID BLUNT

DIARISTS, in the painful experience of any one who has tried to keep a journal upon inadequate material, are made and not born. They are most completely the creatures of circumstance, totally dependent for their merit upon the actual interest of their environment. Thus, any student of Swinburne knows that a man may write lyrics of the high seas in Putney; and a recent observer actually saw William Morris composing epic poems with what the divorce lawyers would call a Hammersmith domicil. But if a man's diary is to be anything beyond an anxiety to his grandchildren, he must live in the world. One has suffered too long under this sort of thing:

Sunday.—Drove this morning to Newington Butts to see the fresh primroses. How wonderful Nature is, to be sure. We dined with William. Walter was there with his young wife, and a Mr. Babbage, of the Poor Law Board; very entertaining. Jane found him extremely genteel, for a public functionary. He says that Palmerston's Government is riding for a fall, and that Lord John is in high hopes. I wonder.

That is perhaps why one winces a little at every new announcement that another diary is to be torn from its legitimate retreat in the mahogany bureau under the bust of Charles James Fox and thrust, mildly protesting, into publicity.

A diary, as such, possesses no more intrinsic interest than an antique. But if either of these objects, in addition to being an original journal or genuine Chippendale, happens to possess charm or beauty or unpublished points of view, its exhibition is one of the best things that can happen to the discoverer. The diary of Mr. Wilfrid Blunt, reinforced by his later comments and explanations, belongs easily to this fortunate class; and it deserves a better fate than that evisceration by hasty journalistic persons in search of anecdotes about well-known people, which is the normal destiny of reprinted journals. The writer of it moved with an air of graceful and distinguished eccentricity through the semi-political *monde* of the Nineties and escaped, by reason of his social position, those dreary and uninforming dinners with William, Walter and his young wife to which I have already referred. His set was adorned on the political side by the Radical members of Mr. Gladstone's last Government, by young George Wyndham and young George Curzon, who "was, as usual, the most brilliant; he never flags for an instant either in speech

or repartee" (*quantum mutatus ab illo Hectore*), and
—one almost gropes for the more impressive inter-
lineated "and" of the theatre programme which intro-
duces the Leading Lady—Miss Margot Tennant.
She first appears like a female Paris (and both the
arbitrator and the capital city of that name are essentially feminine) awarding the apple between "her
political admirers, Haldane and Asquith"; then after
her engagement to "a little smooth-shaved middle-
aged man, with a beatific smile on his face, as of one
to whom Heaven's doors have been opened"; and
finally on the wedding day, when "Margot was pale,
very pale, but firm and decided, Asquith much
smartened up." There are moments when Mr.
Blunt's *Mémoires pour servir à l'histoire de mon
temps* positively rise to the interest of a Society
paper, when his old Adam approximates to the
young, contemporary *Eve*.

As no well-informed diary *de nos jours* would be
complete without a new and thoroughly authentic
narrative of the dismal *crime passionel* of the late
Crown Prince Rudolph, Mr. Blunt conscientiously
presents posterity with a version of the Meyerling
story that is even newer and more authentic than
usual. He listened to William Morris shouting down
the bargees of the Upper Thames and enjoying that
advantage which *bourgeois* poets must always possess

in contests of pure imagination, until this country
achieves a real equality of educational opportunity.
And he is thoroughly in the fashion for depreciating
the personal equipment of Meredith, whom he found
"a queer, voluble creature, with a play-acting voice,
and conversation like one dictating to a secretary, a
constant search for epigrams."

An earlier journal, which Mr. Blunt kept in Paris
during the hot weather of 1870, forms a most interesting addition to the book. He watched from the
angle of the British Embassy the gradual clouding
of the European sky; and he heard the bursting of
the Prussian storm with the small-minded enjoyment
of an Orleanist, who could not resist his satisfaction
at the slow stumbles of Napoleon III, as he went
wearily to his fall. So small was his sympathy with
the dynasty that he was apparently under the impression that Rouher, the *Vice-Empereur* who had
governed France for a decade, was named "Rouère."
Mentana, the triumph of the *chassepot,* appears under a singularly Trans-atlantic disguise as "Mon-
tana"; and Mr. Gladstone's thoroughly effective intervention in favour of Belgian neutrality is dismissed
as "that absurd Belgian treaty." It is a form of absurdity to which British statesmanship has been hon-
ourably prone.

But the bulk of the volume is filled with the subject of which Mr. Blunt is, from his own angle, an acknowledged master—Egypt. The iniquity of the British occupation, the Machiavellianism of Evelyn Baring, and the astute journalism of Alfred Milner form a background to the whole picture of Mr. Blunt and his contemporaries. The long mutter of his resentment against the slow unfolding of the Imperialist design in Africa is like the drone of the bagpipes under the air which he plays. Wherever he looked in the Nineties he found "the white scramble for Africa" in its undignified and never-receding progress. Egypt, Morocco, Uganda, and Rhodesia each had their turn; and Mr. Blunt's outspoken advocacy was always equally at the disposal of *fellahin* and Matabele. His narrative of Egyptian events forms a most valuable *apparatus criticus* to Lord Cromer's *Modern Egypt;* and apart from its historical merit, his journal is the fine and enduring presentation of a fearless and honourable career.

P. T. BARNUM

THE modern world, as we have learnt to call the pleasing welter of motor omnibuses and telephone calls in which we live, may be distinguished from its predecessors by one peculiar accomplishment. It would appear to the scared observer of contemporary conditions that Publicity (for which Mr. Babbitt had a shorter and more expressive name) is the leading contribution of our age to the slow ascent of Man towards the stars. The traveller approaching a classical, a mediæval, and even a Renaissance city was made aware of its position by the slow heave of its silhouette above the skyline. The square bulk of a citadel, a line of walls, the thrust of towers against the sky were all that told him, as he came across the plain, that the city was in sight. No hoarding insisted hoarsely that the Temple of Æsculapius would cure That Sinking Feeling. No ingenious arrangement of slats insinuated (when approached from the right) that Roger Bacon had at last discovered and was prepared to part, on reasonable terms, with the Elixir of Life, or (viewed from the left) that another of Fra Savonarola's Outspoken Articles would appear on Sunday. There were no announcements that the paintings in the Sistine Chapel were now on view, no intimations that the First Folio of Shakespeare was now on sale. These things happened in a total and, as it seems to our deafened ears, almost an unnatural silence. With his eyes unassailed by any explosion of Publicity, the traveller came on across the plain towards the city, and its towers climbed slowly up the sky.

Not so the modern city. In quiet fields fifty miles out of town the nervous visitor may read the names of its products in letters nine feet high. Then he begins to get his umbrella down and to sit expectantly with his bag on his knees; for he knows that he is coming into the city. Its goods, so to speak, are all in the shop window. Indeed many of them appear hardly content to stay there quietly under glass, awaiting public notice. They seem to leap out at the prospective purchaser with loud indications of quality and profuse gestures of explanation. They buttonhole him in the street; they accost him in the suburbs; they go half-way out into the country to meet him with shrill announcements of their high, their unsurpassable merit.

This bright example has been followed by the entire community. Poets roar their own praises through

megaphones at patient audiences. Statesmen hasten
to write their own biographies, lest any less reverent
hand should be laid on their reputations. And actors,
rarely backward in public insistence upon their own
peculiar merit, stare bewildered at the blazing publicity of Deans and Chapters. It is the modern note,
the thing that lends its peculiar flavour to our age.
We may hope that posterity will study our pictures
or read our poetry. But it is far more probable that
it will collect our advertisements.

Foremost among the founders of that peculiar
church, high among the Pilgrim Fathers of that remarkable quest stands a strange figure with far too
many ruffles on its shirt-front and a large diamond
stud, a tall old gentleman who managed to combine
obesity with height, who patted children on the head,
and told respectful untruths to the Prince of Wales,
who imported Jumbo, invented General Tom Thumb,
and left to proverbial literature the unforgettable
name of P. T. Barnum.

If there is a canon of advertising saints, a Roll
of advertising Honour, a hierarchy of those supreme
Boosters before whose stately (and well displayed)
images the innumerable Babbitts of two continents
prostrate themselves, one may be sure that the figure
of Mr. Barnum is somewhere near the top: he would
have seen to that.

SUPERS AND SUPERMEN

The astonishing career, which opened in the genteel New York of 1835 and ended in the gaze of the
whole civilized world in 1891, was in all its stages a
miracle of publicity. When he tripped over a rope
at eighty in Madison Square Garden and scratched
himself, the old man rose shouting for his press-
agent. And as he lay dying, they asked whether his
feelings would be hurt if an evening paper printed
an obituary. "Not at all" was the answer; and when
he got four columns, the old man's health began to
mend a little. That instinct for advertisement brought
him into bankruptcy and out of it, into the memory
of three generations of children, and on the lips of
civilized mankind, with the trifling exception of those
outlying races to which it was not worth while to send
the Greatest Show on Earth.

It was a strange career, and exquisitely discord-
ant with the prim correctness of the American scene
in 1836. The young man's father was called Philo
F. and his sister was Miss Minerva. When he fell
in love, it was with a young lady named Charity; and
even when he met a travelling showman, he was called
Hackariah. But these austere beginnings were soon
left behind. He beheld New York; and the vacant
expression of a great city waiting to be amused fired
his imagination. An aged negress was procured and
reminded (with some difficulty) that she remembered

George Washington. The public paid; and Barnum had tasted blood. She became the first of a long and glorious line. There was the Fiji Mermaid, who startled polite society in 1842, the Woolly Horse—"extremely complex, made up of the Elephant, Deer, Horse, Buffalo, Camel and Sheep"—and Jumbo, "the Only Mastodon on Earth." There was the Bearded Lady and the Dog-faced Boy. There was General Thumb and Miss Jenny Lind. It is an astounding dynasty.

There is something pleasing in the blaring progress of Barnum's incredible caravan round the blameless world of the Nineteenth Century. His descent on London in 1844 is full of delightfully unsuitable contrasts. The dwarf was established at a peer's house in Grafton Street, and the Baroness Rothschild gave a party for him. There was even an audience at Buckingham Palace, in the course of which the General conversed with the Prince Consort; and the *Court Circular* reported that "his personation of the Emperor Napoleon elicited great mirth, and this was followed by a representation of the Grecian Statuary, after which the General danced a nautical hornpipe and sang several of his favourite songs." On a later visit the little man sang "Yankee Doodle," to the mild surprise of a Court at which the memory of North American sedition was still recent. He indicated that Majesty might suitably bestow upon him a specimen of that pony upon which his eponymous saint had ridden. But the Queen was unresponsive, and all that the General got was the usual pencil-case: there were still a few in stock when Napoleon III came to Windsor eleven years later, and the Emperor got one for his birthday.

So the odd progress went on. Sometimes Barnum's career seems to call for the simple brush of Mr. Sinclair Lewis, and sometimes for the stranger touch of Mr. Walter de la Mare. For nearly sixty years the big, genial man humbugged his contemporaries. They always saw an extremely good show; but they never saw all that they thought they saw. Perhaps that is the best that any artist can do for his public.

IN MEMORIAM

Lord Kitchener
Mons—Gallipoli
The Irish Guards
Ronald Poulton

LORD KITCHENER

BIOGRAPHY, like big game hunting, is one of the recognized forms of sport; and it is as unfair as only sport can be. High on some far hill-side of politics or history the amateur marks down his distant quarry. Follows an intensely distasteful period of furtive approach to the subject, which leads the deer-stalker up gullies and ravines and the biographer through private letters and washing-books. The burns grow deeper and wetter, the letters take a more private and less publishable turn, until at last our sportsman, well within range, turns to his publisher, who carries the guns, and empties one, two, and (if the public will stand it) three barrels into his unprotesting victim; because it is a cruel truth that the subjects of *Lives* are rarely themselves alive. It is at once the shame of biographers and the guarantee of their marksmanship that they are perpetually shooting the sitting statesman.

But if biography is to have any higher value than mere anecdote, its central figure must bring some-

thing more to the historical imagination than the titil-
lation of scandal or the whisper of revelations. It is
not enough that he should confide to us what the Duke
really said in the Lobby when the Bill was thrown
out, or whether it is true that the Regent upon one
occasion went somewhat further than he was hitherto
believed to have gone. But he must be a person
whose career summarizes in a convenient form the
tone and temper of his age; and that, in a quite surprising degree, does the career of Lord Kitchener.

One had come to regard him so mechanically as
a unique phenomenon in British life. But this fallacy, like so many more, is a legacy of 1914, when a
clean-shaven country swept an anxious hand over
its upper lip in search of some counterpoise to
Hohenzollern and Hindenburg, and found in
Kitchener the one moustache whose dimensions were
sufficiently *sabreur,* the one collar whose altitude was
adequately Teutonic to fill the military bill. The
paragraphists have spoilt our appreciation of him
with their dreary insistence on his Himalayan
solitude. In reality, he was a highly-generalized version of that exquisitely characteristic figure, the Victorian soldier. In his first phase, when Mr. Disraeli
was Prime Minister, one finds in him a rich example
of that blend of soldiering with Christian connoisseurship which rose to its greatest and most baroque

heights in General Gordon. "My dear Miss Conder," he wrote to a brother-officer's sister, "I send you some information about the vestments of the Church of England that you wished to have"; and thereupon he makes such play with Stoles, Albs, Copes, Tunicles, and Chasubles as would do credit to a diocesan conference, and closes upon an arch sectarian joke ("I must now end this popish letter"), whose positively kittenish note would have proceeded more naturally from a pale young curate. In the next chapter he becomes a more popular figure, that might have walked into any magazine story between the year 1885 and the second Jubilee without exciting the reader's suspicion. The scene is perpetually set upon a shifting carpet of burning sand; under the coppery glare of an African sky a few Baggara crouch muttering round a low fire outside a black tent or so; and there is a general feeling that something has been happening beyond Wady Halfa or above the Tenth Cataract or in Darfur or Kordofan. But a tall figure strides in among them. The hair, the dress, the beard are Mahdist enough; but that gesture of command can only be an Englishman's—it is Captain —— of the Frontier Force! That is a popular frame into which almost every picture of Kitchener's early and middle life will fit. He was intensely typical of the Victorian scene; and it is that fact which gives to his long career its real value for the picturesque historian.

Born a few months before the Great Exhibition, when the Prince Consort had eleven years still to live, he enjoyed an education which was the plaything of Irish governesses and the holiday task of a Rugby master. Indeed it may well be that if he had gone nearer to any public school, he would have grown up a less perfect public school boy; the system might have provoked reactions. At the age of thirteen some educational eccentricity of his family directed him to a school near Geneva, and it is a solemn thought that a few years earlier the crocodile in which the gaunt young Kitchener paced might have passed on that Calvinist shore another line of schoolboys, in which ambled, out of step, mildly observant, his head deep in the *Revue des Deux Mondes,* Master Henry James, junior, of Cambridge, Mass. But one doubts, somehow, if an encounter would have led to an intimacy.

Five years later, at Woolwich, he set his foot to the military ladder and diversified his technical studies with the dreadful pastime of reading the Old Testament in Hebrew. Warfare began for him with a flying glimpse of the almost equally flying operations of the Second Army of the Loire in Brittany. The Franco-Prussian War had attracted large numbers of able-bodied Anglo-Saxon sightseers: Sir Charles Dilke had been at Wörth with the Crown Prince, Mr. Labouchere was in Paris with Trochu, and it was only natural that two gentlemen cadets should take train through the snow in search of Chanzy. His service in 1871, which was almost confined to taking pleurisy in a balloon, was rewarded by the issue of a French war-medal in 1913; the delay was a characteristically graceful tribute by the Ministry of War to the methods of British military administration. He was retrieved by an anxious parent, scolded at the Horse Guards by a maternal Commander-in-Chief of the Blood Royal, and finally gazetted to the Royal Engineers.

The army which the Duke of Cambridge commanded for Queen Victoria in her early widowhood can hardly have provided a young enthusiast with an exhilarating arena. While Frenchmen, Germans, Austrians, Italians, and Danes had seen creditable and recent service on the continent of Europe, British soldiers had little beyond doubtful memories of the Crimea to set beside their archaic recollections of the wars against Napoleon. It was a depressing period, in which the Line regiments were provided with an unconvincing imitation of the Prussian helmet, in a vague hope that it would act as an agreeable substitute for the Prussian Staff College. Three years of

Chatham and Aldershot, with an excursion to the Austrian *Kaisermanöver* of 1873, proved thoroughly unsatisfying. Bridging and the field telegraph failed to bind Kitchener to the Engineer's career; and in 1874 that singular young man was loaned to the Palestine Exploration Fund for its survey of the Holy Land. It is possible that he was not precisely such stuff as Schliemanns are made of. But, something of a Hebraist and more of a Bible student, he entered keenly on any work in which the pill of archæology was gilded with the glamour of oriental travel. For eight years he disappeared into the dust of the Levant. His cartography was sometimes leavened with street-fighting; and in 1878 he was honoured with a special summons to Cyprus, in order to survey the latest, if somewhat uncut, diamond which Lord Beaconsfield had added to his astonished sovereign's crown. In the later weeks of the Russo-Turkish War he followed the Turks into Thrace, an exploit which the gyrations of Turkish policy unfortunately prevented him from turning to propagandist account during the war of 1914; and a few years later he almost turned archæologist for life on a proposal of the British Museum that he should excavate in Assyria and Babylonia. This accident, which so nearly happened, resembles that chance which almost sent Mirabeau to commence bookseller in Kiel, and that

other which so nearly promoted General Bonaparte
to the post of instructor in the Turkish artillery.

With the dawn of the Eighties Egypt took the
stage; and until she left it after Omdurman, Kitchener was perpetually in her train. He appears first
as a Bimbashi of Egyptian cavalry, who heightened
its prestige by inventing an incredible light blue uniform; then as a commander of native irregulars and
secret agent in the Korosko and Bayuda Deserts;
and finally as the Sirdar who made the Egyptian
Army, rounded up Osman Digna, and broke the
Khalifa. His Egyptian service had in it a real note
of service for Egypt; and his militarism was never
so military, his Imperialism not half so imperial as the
tone of the men who followed in his wake. His final
biography does much to clear his work from the unpleasant colour with which it had been daubed by such
words as Bishop Brindle's detestable crow of episco-
pal triumph:

> The tribes had taken Dongola, and we had to move them
> out. We did so—thoroughly. They ran for their lives,
> mothers throwing down their babies on the sands, leaving
> them as hostages.

That was never the tone in which Kitchener thought
of his work: perhaps he had not read enough Kipling.

In his next period (it was not his second manner,
because his manner never changed), he finished the

war in South Africa and reorganized the forces in India. As he was a successful, so he was not a romantic soldier; and the man who had substituted railway-lines for heroism in the Sudan preferred barbed wire to grand strategy in Cape Colony. His Indian exploit possesses for connoisseurs of Lord Curzon all the interest which attaches to an Ajax who defied the lightning without ill-effects; and his government of Egypt in the years between the coronation of King George V and the outbreak of war has a considerable provincial importance.

But his career, which had been passed hitherto among coloured peoples, was to acquire suddenly the deeper significance which is inseparable from the direction of a great white State. A man made bad use of a Browning pistol in a back street in Bosnia; the world of white men stood to arms; and Kitchener came to the War Office to serve, so long as he lived, as the first military adviser of the country which he made the first military power in the world. By a queerness of which only Englishmen are capable, his war service has become a subject of controversy. One of our Ciceros, in his anxiety to exhibit himself as the only authorized saviour of the State, has his doubts. One of our conquerors, whose pen, since he exchanged G.H.Q. for the Viceregal Lodge, is unquestionably mightier than his sword, has his misgivings. And what remains? The record of a man who built broad and deep in the first months, and smaller men took the fame of it in the last; who stamped with his foot upon the ground, and men in ranks rose out of it. His achievement is of the order of deeds which men write upon stone. But they do not argue about them.

MONS—GALLIPOLI

THERE is a certain state of mind, unless perhaps it is a state of health, which prefers its hopes forlorn. It can only breathe in the tense air of disaster; and failure has quite a success with it. Any student of opinion will tell you that, with a British posterity, one sound, romantic defeat will go twice as far as three vulgar victories; and nothing in London is more significant than the fact that Gordon, who failed, is in Trafalgar Square, whilst Napier, who succeeded, has penetrated no further than Waterloo Place. Contemporaries may be incommoded by the loss of a war; but posterity, if the historians know their business, is a glutton for failure.

This temper, which is as early as the *Chanson de Roland* and as late as the latest book on the Dardanelles, is not entirely peculiar to these islands; but it is on British territory that it has found its fullest expression. Deriving small satisfaction from the monotonies of military success, and taking little pleasure in the brass and cymbals of triumphant marches, it turns a sensitive ear to catch the wailing minor and the muffled drums as the Lost Legion goes by. It feeds, like some sick bee, upon the shrunken laurels of defeat; and if it has a favourite General, he is probably Sir John Moore. Lord Nelson and, in a smaller degree, Lord Kitchener, humoured it, when they atoned for a career of victory with a death so ill-timed that it was almost as good as a defeat; and even Mr. Kipling, who is at other times a most regular attendant at divine worship on the side of the big battalions, paid an unusual tribute to the British taste for reverses when he dwelt lovingly on the panic of the "Fore and Aft," known to a less chauvinistic *Army List* of the early Nineties as "The Fore and Fit, Princess Hohenzollern-Sigmaringen-Auspach's Merthyr-Tydfilshire Own Royal Loyal Light Infantry."

The mood is a queer one, with its sentimental hankering after frustrated effort. It loves the bridges to go down behind an anxious army; it rejoices as the Matabele come in with the assegai between the white-topped waggons of the *laager;* and it is never so happy as when a British square is broken in the desert south of Korti and the Baggara sweep in, slashing and stabbing round the jammed Gatling. Its taste is all for the half-lights and the subdued tones of unsuccess; and it is, so far as it relates to military failure, a peculiarly British taste. One cannot remember any Roman writer who felt the wistful charm of Carrhae; Jena Day was never widely celebrated in Prussia; and one has not heard that an unduly prominent place is occupied by the Armada in the curriculum of the Spanish primary schools. But an island people is agreeably inclined to apply to land warfare romantic canons by which it would never dream of measuring failure in the more serious fields of commerce or war by sea. There is no spot-light of romance centred on heroic bankrupts or unsuccessful admirals. It is only on land that the English display this engaging temper of retrospective defeatism.

Four years of war have inevitably provided this mood with some highly promising raw material. There is a queer tendency in the purveyors of our war literature to prefer the stormy romance of Mons and the sunlit tragedy of Gallipoli to the simpler, more direct appeal of victory in Palestine and Mesopotamia or the decisive triumphs of the French summer of 1918. The historical instinct is a sound one, when it focusses the attention of posterity upon the opening moves in the great game; and there is, besides the sentimental appeal of it, a real importance in the growing literature of Mons and the Marne. The history of Europe for a generation to come, and perhaps the life

of mankind in the whole future which remains to
it, was profoundly modified by the events of that
hot harvest-time of 1914, when the fine flower of German military education drew a bow at anything but
a venture, and missed.   It is true that it took the
Allies four years to win the war which the Germans
had lost in 1914; but the history of any month of
those four years which followed is of less significance
than the story of any half-hour in the six weeks
which had gone before.

General Lanrezac's story is in many ways the most
illuminating. One begins in it at the very beginning,
when the wires were still humming between the European capitals with solutions of the Servian *impasse.*
A roomful of Generals sat round a table in the Rue
St. Dominique, and an imperturbable old gentleman
with a heavy moustache smiled indomitably (and even
a trifle irritatingly) at his anxious questioners.   One
General came away from the conference asking fret-
fully whether Joffre "had an idea"; and one is left
with an uneasy feeling that if he had, it was the idea
of Wilkins Micawber.   It is desolating to realize that
upon these frivolous old gentlemen, with their false
mystery and their half-developed "science" of war,
rested the continued existence of European democracy.   No spectacle of equal inadequacy was presented to mankind until the meeting of the Peace Con-

ference nearly five years later, when the pigmies went mud-larking round the foundations of the New Jerusalem.

After this vivid glimpse of an August afternoon in Paris, the story deepens; and one has the torturing spectacle of French Headquarters straining their eyes eastwards for the dust of the German advance, whilst the fevered Lanrezac on the Belgian frontier insisted in tones of increasing asperity that the danger lay in the North. At this point the Germans take up the tale; and General von Kluck takes station on the right of the German line to sweep across Belgium, swing half-left, and then, shepherding an unwilling flock before him, to drive down from the frontier into the heart of France. He struck and failed; and the story of that failure is told by him in the level tones of an official memorandum, drafted in 1915 and revised three years later, at a time when there was still a German Empire and a legend of Teutonic invincibility, but a deposed Army commander might strike a more impressive attitude in the theatre of posterity by transferring a little blame to Great Headquarters.

It is the function of the technical military historian to undramatize the most dramatic events in history; he could probably reduce *King Lear* to an appreciation of the general situation on the Heath, operation orders of the French army, and a despatch from the Earl of Kent to the Secretary of State for War. General von Kluck has purged his drama of all its pity and all its terror with more than Aristotelian thoroughness; and one would hardly guess, without looking at the place names, that the even voice with its Staff College pedantry was telling the tale of that incredible August, when men fought all day and marched all night and remade a world in the white dust of the French roads. It all reads so like the report of an Army Inspector on the autumn manœuvres of 1912, that one waits automatically for the crashing charge of massed cavalry with which a courtly Staff generally titillated the military imagination of Imperial Majesty; and one starts at the sudden discovery of a real enemy killing and being killed, and a *finale* on the Marne which owed nothing to German stage-management.

The story of Mons found a happy ending on the Marne. But Gallipoli marches towards its catastrophe like the *Agamemnon*. In the first act lighthearted warships slide up and down a blue sea, tossing shell into nineteenth-century forts. Follows a pause, in which an amiable gentleman took orders in a room in Whitehall; and then a party of Generals found themselves installed in a cruiser to watch the Navy batter its head against the Narrows and draw

off, with the little ships huddled round the mined,
lop-sided battleships. Then came an interlude to
martial music in Egypt, when Sir Ian, thoroughly
attuned to the historical significance of his command,
took the salute at a review in the sand outside Alex-
andria and went home to write in his diary: "High,
high soared our hopes. Jerusalem—Constantinople?" But the answer to his eager question was—
Gallipoli.

His diary is, on the whole, the best document that
has come out of the war. When he followed the
Japanese in Manchuria as a mere Military Attaché,
he managed to convey more of the meaning of war
in *A Staff Officer's Scrap Book* than any writer
on it since Tolstoi; and when the commander of the
Mediterranean Expeditionary Force turns its historian, he writes not only the best book on the war
but, in one judgment, the best book on war. His
Odyssey (for, like Odysseus, Sir Ian Hamilton was
born in the Ionian Islands) is a brilliant achievement.
He has a keen eye for detail and a vivid historical
imagination; and his grasp of the general contours
of the wood does not disable him from pointing out
the amusing shape of many of the trees. Indeed it
is the vivid drawing of his details which helps burn the
whole picture into one's memory. Lord Kitchener
at his desk "with flashing spectacles"; the conning-

tower of the *Queen Elizabeth* during the landing on
the Peninsula; those awful boats off Ocean Beach
("Several boats are stranded along this no man's
land; so far all attempts to get out at night and bury
the dead have only led to fresh losses. No one ever
landed out of these boats, so they say"); and the night
sounds at sea ("Half an hour the bombardment and
counter-bombardment, and then there arose the
deadly crepitation of small-arms—no messages—ten
times I went back and forward to the signal-room—
no messages—until a new and dreadful sound was
carried on the night wind out to sea—the sound
of the shock of whole regiments—the Turkish Allah
Din!—our answering loud Hurrahs")—such pictures
as these are raw, living history written down by a
man who helped to make it. The literary accomplishment of them may scandalize the illiterate taci-
turnity of some of our conquerors. But Gallipoli was
not lost because Sir Ian could write English: one
should never forget that Napoleon, who was as successful as most Sandhurst soldiers, talked incessantly
from birth and produced thirty-two volumes of correspondence.

The history of the affair appears pitiably clear
from Sir Ian's journal. First, the soldiers were put
in to watch the sailors win. Then submarines thrust
their grey snouts into the blue waters of the Levant,

and the sailors, their skirts tucked tightly round their
ankles, stood by to watch the soldiers win. They
did not win in the first chapter, because Sir John
French was going to end the war at Loos and required for that purpose the entire resources of the
British Empire. They did not win in the second
chapter, because Mr. Lloyd George had discovered,
by the aid of a small-scale map, that the war was
to be won in the suburbs of Salonika, and the Government diverted to the aid of Serbia the men who
might have marched into Constantinople. It is a
queer story that Sir Ian tells, between his official
correspondence and his etchings of war. In his gracious retrospect Gallipoli, for all the horror of its failure and its unburied dead, is touched with an odd
quality that is almost charm, drawn from a thousand
friendships and ten thousand sacrifices. "How sad
and mad and bad it was—But then, how it was
sweet!"

I

No one except the village cad criticizes the village War Memorial. Its sentiment may be second-rate; its material may be shoddy; its execution may be frankly local. But the little horror of monumental masonry which interrupts the village green is something more than an expression of the inartistic impulse of its creator. It is an embodiment, a rather pitiable little effigy of real men deserving to be honoured. They cannot now speak for themselves; and if they could, they would undoubtedly say something quite different. But that clumsy figure, that far too Celtic cross is a halting attempt to put them on record; and one does not complain if it is sometimes a little out of drawing.

In that aspect when Mr. Kipling's piety erected a sort of Cenotaph in honour of the Irish Guards, he was above criticism; and one can only pass it with the appropriate gesture of respect. It is a full and detailed picture of an interminable procession of young men, which passed by under the shifting light of war for four years. There is hardly time to catch many of the faces as they go past; and the picture seems almost to be drawn with that queer lack of perspective which gave their charm to those panoramic rolls of coloured paper that used to be sold in the streets at Coronation times. But the long line of young men stands out clearly; and there is a full record of the dismal round of trenches, raids, billets, great offensives, camps, and fatigues which made up the life of two Battalions of Foot Guards in the long, slow interval between the sunny evening near Harmignies, when a stray bullet hit the Belgian turf and someone said, "Now we can say we have been under fire," and the driving rain and gleaming pavements of Cologne, with a General sitting his horse to watch them go by, and the drums pounding out "Brian Boru."

The record should satisfy the men (there are none too many of them) who came through. And perhaps it may give something back to the groping memories of those who are waiting, still waiting to talk it all over with some who are slower to return. It is for them, and for the father of "Lieut. J. Kipling (missing)," that the book was written.

II

Yet it has another aspect. As a memorial to the Irish Guards, it is above comment. But as Mr. Kipling's contribution to the history of the War, it is vastly more interesting. That sudden reputation, which startled our fathers into a dazed recognition of a new writer of English prose, was largely made by a *staccato* familiarity with war. In the later years of the last century Mr. Kipling became a prose Laureate of the British Army. He learnt its idiom in dusty cantonments beyond Bombay; and he dispensed its adventures to the civilian public in short, sharp doses. Gradually it became uncertain whether he had described or invented its leading types; and Aldershot became a training-ground where men qualified for participation in some vivid *scenario* of his above the Sixth Cataract or in the throat of the Khyber Pass.

That is why one waited, when a real war came, for Mr. Kipling to write about it. At first his utterance was a trifle impeded by the exigencies of propaganda or the stammer of genuine indignation. He prophesied smooth things about the training-camps of the New Army. He grimaced in verse at—

"The Pope, the swithering Neutrals,
The Kaiser and his Gott"—

and, on one occasion, which an unkind War Savings Association has perpetuated in print, he said quite a number of highly remarkable things to an audience at Folkestone. But these deliverances (and it is hardly fair to disinter them) were little more than the flying arrows of a busy propagandist. One had to wait until the war had dropped back into some sort of perspective before Mr. Kipling, or anyone else, could write about it.

He has chosen to paint an enormous panorama of one tiny section of the front line. He has drawn it in infinite detail, and with hardly an omission of any insignificant or sickening particular. One gets the Retreat, and a swarm of hornets at Villers Cotterêts, and the gun-horse that trod on a big drum at Landrecies, and First Ypres, and the dead man in the road at Zillebeke, and Neuve Chapelle, and the Somme, and a mine-crater full of horrors near St. Pierre Vaast, and the miracle of ownerless rum-jars at Gouzeaucourt, and the night when Mr. —— asked the Sergeant and the dead man if it was "all cosy down there," and the March Push, and a horse show, and the last battles. It is all like that. Almost every episode from Mons to Cologne is described lovingly and with equal emphasis. Mr. Kipling has deliberately abandoned perspective and has substituted for it the indiscriminate inclusion of friendly reminis-

310

cences. To the men who lived through it every incident was an incident to remember, and they have helped Mr. Kipling to remember it. The result is a queer collection of vivid detail, which reminds one a little in its precision of those huge and minute panoramas of French soldiers under fire in which Alphonse de Neuville used to record the details of war in 1870.

Mr. Kipling is happiest in his detail, even when it is unpleasant. After a lifetime spent in reducing the contents of his note-books to the unhandy form of fiction, he has manifestly enjoyed examining witnesses and transcribing their depositions bodily on to the page. By a queer irony the majority of them appear to have insisted upon talking in the idiom which they had learnt from his earlier works. His reported conversations are authentic beyond a doubt. But one recognizes with a shock of surprise in Mr. Kipling's reminiscent Guardsman the jerky, italicized emphasis of "The Infant" and his friends (... "but what *I* mean to say is that if it hadn't been for those two dam' sheets" . . . .). Or the deeper, more familiar accents of Mulvaney himself: " 'Tis against Nature for a man to be buried with his breath in him." Or the reminiscent gambit of "My kit was all new, too, me bein' back from leave. Our C.S.M. drew me attention to it one of those merry nights we was poachin' about in No Man's Land. ' 'Tis a pity,' says he, 'you did not bring the band from Caterham *also*,' says he. ' 'Twould have amused Jerry.' My new kit was shqueakin' an' clickin' the way they could have heard it a mile. Ay, Gouzeaucourt an' the trenches outside Gonnelieu." . . . Or even the full glories of the anecdotic manner: "Rivers round Maubeuge? 'Twas *all* rivers" . . . until one half expects Learoyd to turn heavily on his back in the shade, as the little Ortheris spits wearily into the ditch of a sun-baked Indian fort.

Sometimes (but not often) he permits his reader the luxury of a passage of description. For the most part of his long journey he is content to amble along on the day-to-day happenings of the Battalions. But once or twice, generally in the neighbourhood of Ypres, his imagination takes charge, and the Orderly Room drone of his routine narrative gives way to a burst of prose. There is a strange haunting picture of the broken town itself ("The way most of us took it, was we felt 'twas The Fear itself—"), and a sheaf of vivid etchings of life (and death) under fire.

His vocabulary has lost none of its old violence. Things chatter and slither and rip, whilst human beings caper and plowter alongside, in the strange idiom in which he has conveyed sound and movement for a generation past. But the whole unending panorama which he has presented is still an impressive thing. There is a great wealth of detail; and sometimes it has all the dulness of great wealth. The tedium of war is sometimes conveyed by a corresponding tedium of narrative. But the broad picture remains.

The weakness is that the painter brings his picture too close to the eye; and so there is no perspective. His reader is left, a little helpless, to sort it all out for himself. After that is done, one remembers hardly a fault, except an ungenerous kick at John Redmond and an aimless, nagging dissatisfaction with civilians for neglecting to prepare for war on a scale which no single soldier in Europe had foreseen. But one need not bandy politics with Mr. Kipling across his Cenotaph.

III

For, in the last resort, that is the aspect of this book which must remain. He wrote it for the two Battalions and for their people. It is a fine possession, which they will not criticise.

RONALD POULTON

I

I CAN remember Ronald Poulton (and one is left now with memories instead of friends) in his first term at Rugby. The little scene was set between the bare trees and brick walls of Caldecott's playing-field on a half-holiday afternoon in the late autumn of 1903. One can almost recover the pleasurable air of privileged loafing with which one celebrated a temporary exemption from games, parading the six-foot way between the different grounds, watching the gratifying exertions of other people, and wearing such mufflers and overcoats as almost made one believe in the failing health to which one owed the rest. Someone who was well informed about the School House (and its contents were as much a special subject as the Balkan races) said that they had a new man who was a fast three-quarter. He gave his name, and pointed out a lean boy with the figure of a ferret, who detached himself for an instant from the scramble of Whites and Stripes. That was the first that some of us saw of Ronald Poulton.

In the following term the Sports must have lifted him out of the ruck of little boys in large collars, and people began to know his name. He rose from Caldecott's to Bigside (I suppose that he never descended with most of us to Benn's), and the swerving run with the rigid, down-stretched arms moving from side to side before him became as familiar as the flat strike of the School clock. Out of games, he was soon lost to sight in the mysterious region of the Science Specialists, whom one knew only as a confused noise in the Arnold Library. The School House of those days (and of these, for all that I know) made almost a criminal offence of acquaintance with the outside world, so that one was not permitted to know him until he had climbed above the clouds into the calm air of the Sixth, where one could visit other people's houses and speak to them without the fear of prosecution. Then in the autumn of 1907, when he and Watson were double Captains of the XV like the two kings of Sparta, a new and nervous Head of the School found in the athletes his loyal and indispensable secular arm. Together we manipulated the voting of Bigside Levée, that singularly unmanageable popular assembly, whose decrees

were necessary for the variation of a hat band or
the purchase of a Sports cup. One appealed to him
for the support of his smile, which carried almost
more votes than his prestige, and of the big battalions
of the School House; and in return one used the
authority of the Chair to get him wholly unjusti-
fiable adjournments when the prospects of a division on his motions seemed unpromising. There
was a particularly sinister occasion early in 1908,
when he opposed a revolutionary proposal "that
members of the Running VIII in their second year
be permitted to wear a white straw hat"; as the House
looked friendly to the proposal, "the Chairman ad-
journed the Levée without putting the question, in
view of the fact that only a small proportion of the
Upper School was present"; and a more carefully
constituted House rejected the heresy five days later.
His support in Sixth Levée, a Second Chamber with
a deplorable tendency to independence, gave one the
votes of distant Specialists and remote inhabitants
of the Army Class; and in our last year it saved the
administration from defeat on a grave proposal that
someone should suffer for the delightful offence of
reading the Second Lesson in batting-gloves for a bet
of two shillings. There was also assistance rendered
in other directions; the Upper Bench had decided
to vary the intolerable calm of First Lesson with an

alarm clock, which was to be set for **7.25 a.m.** and placed in the little gallery round Old Sixth School. As the Upper Bench, a grave assembly of Heads of Houses and scholars elect of half a dozen Colleges, wished to swear by the card that they had not done it themselves, Poulton was brought in from the Specialists after early Chapel and persuaded to lay the mine. It exploded to time; but the results, on balance, were disappointing.

He seems, as one turns over memories, to have been everywhere in those days. One sees him in the winter, swerving up Bigside to score a try, as the droning chant of "School" jumped into the major key, and the crowd strained forward against the line of beating canes to follow his run up the ground; one sees him in the summer, smiling through cricket "foreigns," which one came out of Third Lesson to look at; and in the snowy springtime of the Sports, sprinting inimitably or helping a nervous fellow-steward to adjust the insidious complications of the School revolver. He appears in light blue cricket caps, in tasselled football caps with the lining sewn full of the names of stricken fields, in hat bands of every imaginable colour and distinction; playing steward at School concerts at the end of Term in the statutory button-hole, which fags brought up in state from the florist's in High Street; and even lecturing to the Natural History Society (whose principal interest was the ecclesiastical architecture of Warwickshire in its relation to illicit smoking) on the Roman Wall, which he had learnt in the holidays with a friend among the House-masters. He was in every picture; but no one could ever persuade him to stand in the centre of it.

II

Oxford, which began for most of us with a dispiriting week of scholarship papers at the end of an autumn term, was not a new land for him, as he had a home and his "last school" there. But he sat for the examination at the long tables in Balliol Hall, scrambled with the rest of us for that queer afternoon tea, which the Master and Fellows gave one as a sedative with the papers, and went back to Rugby with the Science Exhibition that he had come to fetch.

When he came up in 1908, he went into ground-floor rooms in the Garden Quad, which were known to historians to lie near the Dean's forcing-house of First Classes, and were believed by explorers to be on the way to the Laboratory. It was the custom of those days (I am speaking of the reign of Edward VII) for men of the same year to lunch in groups. As there was a singularly unwholesome tradition that lunch was a meal consisting of marmalade and cigarettes, conversation was the staple article of diet; and the selection of one's companions became a matter of more importance than the choice of dishes. For a year he lunched with a big dark man from Rossall who talked, a round fair man from Repton who smiled, and another Rugbeian from the Front Quad who made speeches. There was a rule at that table that no one should talk any one else's "shop"; one was not permitted to know or to show that one knew that he was being tried (it was a remote age) for the University, or that the Union was debating Mr. Asquith's proposals to abolish unemployment (it was a very remote age) by the promiscuous engagement of supernumerary postmen. The sole intrusion of athletics was an occasion on which the other Rugbeian was caught for a College Littleside and found himself without a striped jersey; he appealed for Ronald's and made a short but striking appearance on the Master's Field in the red and white stripes of the School House with a sinister black skull and cross-bones on the left breast, a singularly harrowing experience for a nature which, on the football field at least, was always retiring.

Ronald was always (it explains his one hostility and a good proportion of his friendships) a Rugbeian. There was a dinner to an old Head-master and a tea to a new one whilst he was at Oxford, in which he was inevitably prominent; and I think that a newly-elected President of the Union was never so proud as when a canvasser (canvassing was strictly prohibited) reported ruefully that Ronald, on being reminded of a Rugbeian candidature, had almost killed him for the suggestion that he could possibly have forgotten it.

III

I think that he was the most honest man I ever knew. If he had wished to pretend, he would not have known how to do it; and there was no affectation in him. He played games without *panache* and worked without false solemnity. Some of us have hoped that he was typical of a single school; but we were wrong, because the best is never typical.

He was (it is useless to try to sketch him with a pen, and one is writing for the people who remember) himself; and there is a smile and a voice and a friend that some of them will never forget. There was a facetious undergraduate wrote of him eight years ago: "He has played for England against

RONALD POULTON

France, Ireland, and Scotland: as he is a member of the O.T.C., we trust he will never be required for his country against Germany." It is of no use to wish that wish now.